GENERATION WE

generation We

The Power + Promise of Gen Z

AnneMarie Hayek

LIONCREST
PUBLISHING

GENERATION WE
The Power and Promise of Gen Z

ISBN   978-1-5445-2314-9 *Hardcover*
           978-1-5445-2313-2 *Paperback*
           978-1-5445-2312-5 *Ebook*

FOR

ISABEL

&

SIENA

Contents

Part I

The Roots of Their Power

Introduction

On January 20, 2021, National Youth Poet Laureate Amanda Gorman read her poem "The Hill We Climb" on the steps of the US Capitol to mark the inauguration of President Joe Biden. Biden was the oldest man ever sworn in as president; Gorman was the youngest-ever inaugural poet—and the youngest speaker by far among the day's dignitaries. As the chill wind whipped at her words, this young Black woman, raised by a single mother, saddled with a debilitating speech impediment, stood before the world commanding in her carriage. Only a week after rioters stormed the Capitol threatening our very democratic republic, this diminutive figure called out our nation for its flaws, while simultaneously creating a vision for a better collective future: "There is always light, if only we're brave enough to see it. If only we're brave enough to be it."

Gorman's poem was a sensation. It offered unity after a divisive election campaign, hope after a year of a national pandemic, a vision of collaboration in the midst of a broken political system.

It made her internationally famous. It made her a spokesperson for her generation: Generation Z.

Born in 1998, Gorman was just twenty-two when she used her poem to assert Gen Z's commitment to action: "We know our inaction and inertia will be the inheritance of the next generation."

Gorman had brought the voice of Generation Z to the steps of power, and its clarity of vision to a muddled nation. As she later told the BBC, "I really wanted to use my words to be a point of unity and collaboration." Gen Z sees their choices as starkly as Gorman laid them out. They face a simple binary: unity, collaboration, and bold action now or detrimental inertia that could continue for generations.

This book is about the bold actions Zs are taking—and what they will mean for the rest of us.

FINDING A VOICE

Gen Z has come a long way in finding its voice in a very short time. Just three years ago, few Americans had even heard of Gen Z. Now a Z stood on the biggest platform in the land, speaking truth to power.

Unity, collaboration, and bold action have been the touchstones of Gen Z since they first spoke out as a generation in February 2018, outside Marjory Stoneman Douglas High School in Parkland, Florida. Three days earlier, a shooting had killed seventeen students at the school. Now, high school senior Emma Gonzalez addressed a rally of the victims' fellow students and called bullshit on older generations.

Challenging those who dismissed the voice and demands of their generation, Emma repeated six times, "We call BS."

Emma's peers joined in.

The kids at Parkland didn't believe they could leave the response to what had happened in their school to politicians, community leaders, or well-meaning administrators. They were going to lead themselves. They were sick of school shootings, sick of the empty offers of prayers, sick of political corruption, and sick of apologists.

They were going to speak for themselves. And they were going to make sure that their words were heard.

There are moments when the normal flow of time catches, hesitates, shifts direction by a tiny inflection. This was one of those moments, as a whole generation stepped up to take responsibility for their own lives.

Within four days of the shooting, twenty Parkland students, including Emma Gonzalez and David Hogg, fired up Twitter accounts, blanketed social media with the hashtag #NeverAgain, created their own PAC for gun control, and announced a nationwide March for Our Lives on the one month anniversary of the tragedy. On March 24, 2018, as many as 2 million people protested for gun control in Washington, DC, and at 880 sister events around the country. Students across the country walked out of their classrooms and took to the streets of cities and towns from coast to coast. Most of these protesters were as young as the organizers.

All the March for Our Lives speakers at the Capitol were high schoolers or younger. The two youngest were nine-year-old Yolanda Renee King (Martin Luther King's granddaughter) and eleven-year-old Naomi Wadler. A fifth-grader from Virginia,

Naomi was worried she was "going to mess up" as she stood before a nation, live-streaming her words on Facebook, Twitter, and YouTube. She spoke for all Black girls who had been lost to gun violence and ignored by the media: "We might still be in elementary school, but we know. We know life isn't equal for everyone. And we know what's right and wrong. We also know that we stand in the shadow of the Capitol. And we know that we have seven short years until we, too, have the right to vote." Then-senator Kamala Harris shared a video clip of Wadler's speech. The fifth-grader's plea went viral and became a rallying cry for millions.

March for Our Lives was the largest youth led demonstration since the Vietnam War and one of the largest in US history. And it was organized by kids.

In the face of school shooting after school shooting with little reaction from those in power, a new generation had mobilized.

This was just the start. Suddenly, the voice of youth was impossible to silence. This generation mobilized in record-smashing numbers to demand climate action in the fall of 2019 and racial justice in summer 2020.

But March for Our Lives was the first time many Americans noticed Generation Z. Today, it suddenly feels like Zs are the most visible generation in the country, even though its youngest members won't come of age until 2028. We see Zs in the streets, taking a knee for racial equity and criminal justice reform. We see Zs all over social media demanding immediate action on climate. We sign work emails with pronoun preferences because of their gender inclusivity.

GENERATION WE

Generation Z refers to youth born between 1997 and 2010—I'll talk more later about why this generation is bookended by these particular dates—following the sequence begun by Generation X (1965–1980) and Generation Y (1981–1996).

The Ys are generally known as millennials, and Zs also deserve a more specific name. Something that speaks to their powerful, collective nature and their fierce desire to work together for change. Something that suggests that even if they can't solve all of these problems as a generation, they're hell-bent on trying.

They know they're living at an inflection point. It's one of those rare occasions when there's a real opportunity—albeit a vanishingly small one when it comes to issues like climate—to achieve meaningful change.

I call them Generation We. We've seen ample evidence of their ability to mobilize and work together: they're all about unity, collaboration, and bold action. They have come of age in a time of crises that threaten everyone—climate crisis, racial division, political extremism—and they believe such threats can only be met by a collective reaction.

There's been some recent criticism around Zs' desire to "save the world." And it's true that such claims are little more than puffery. But that's not the real story. To believe that Zs are simply youthful idealists—as other generations were when they were young but later outgrew—is wrong. If anything, Gen Z are the complete opposite of idealists: they're hardened realists driven by evidence that those in positions of authority have not done enough to solve the problems facing our world.

To dismiss Gen Z as the latest teenage Pollyannas, sitting in circles wistfully singing "Imagine," also fails to recognize that they possess tools no other generation has had. Technology has linked them since early in their lives, and they're the first generation to truly harness the power of social media. That gives Generation We unprecedented potential to revolutionize almost every aspect of life and society.

That's the point.

It doesn't really matter whether older generations understand Zs or not—though I'd argue that most do not. It doesn't really matter whether older generations dismiss Zs as idealists or not— though I would argue that most do. The fact is that whatever older generations think, *everyone's* future will be significantly shaped by Zs' bold ideas and actions.

The process has already started.

That's why this isn't just a book about "understanding" Generation Z (and in any case, Zs frankly couldn't give a damn whether older generations understand them or not). Zs see their contemporaries starting to take the reins of power and influence. They're already looking ahead to the world their own generation will shape. This book isn't an introduction to Zs. It goes way beyond introductions to look at the remarkable impact Zs will have, because their impact is going to dominate the rest of the twenty-first century and beyond.

EXTRAORDINARY TIMES

For the last two decades, social researchers have been largely preoccupied with millennials, who, until recently, were the largest generation of Americans.

They were looking in the wrong direction.

Generation We is even larger than the millennials. Zs numbered 86 million in the United States in 2019, predicted to grow to 88 million due to migration over the next two decades.[1] That's more than a quarter of all Americans and more than the combined populations of the two most populous states, California and Texas.

To put it another way, Zs could fill New York City ten times over.

The size of Generation We alone wouldn't necessarily matter if its impact wasn't magnified by its remarkable unity.

Although every generation contains a huge variety of individuals with different perspectives (and Zs are no exception), they are a product of the world that shaped them during their formative years. This shared life experience impacts a generation's worldview, their values, and their aspirations. And the world in which Zs are coming of age is one that calls them to action.

It's not that Zs were born extraordinary, as is sometimes suggested. It's more that their times have made them extraordinary. This is a pivotal period for so many critical issues and the following decades will bring unparalleled change—with Zs at its center.

It's partly an accident of timing, because Zs are coming of age at an inflection point. Whereas it's fair to say that every generation brings change to a greater or lesser degree, this kind of pivot is of a different order. No one knows what comes next, apart from the fact that it's not more of the same. That's why now is the

---

1   "Population Division: World Population Prospects 2019," United Nations, population.un.org/wpp/.

right time to look closely at Zs; it's *their* ideas that will largely shape our trajectory.

For now, Zs are most visible around the issues they see as non-negotiable: climate change, gender, gun regulation and racial equity. Their impact is rapidly spreading.

As this book will explore, their impact will change what we buy and how we work, how we dress, how corporations act, how we educate our kids, and how we vote. It will make us more accountable for what we say and do. It will make us speak more thoughtfully and think more inclusively.

Before 2018, Generation We was barely visible. Now Black Lives Matter (BLM) and the fight for racial equity is on track to become the largest movement in US history—up to 26 million people participated in BLM in the summer of 2020[2]—and Zs are taking a leadership role. Take Nupol Kiazolu, for example, who became the president of BLM Greater New York at just eighteen years old. More than 90 percent of Zs support BLM, and 77 percent have attended at least one BLM protest.[3] We see Zs returning to the streets again and again. We see Zs pushing the movement forward on social media as an ongoing imperative.

Generation We is accelerating a gender revolution, and it goes way beyond the use of pronouns like she/her, he/him, and they/them. Zs are dispensing with traditional gender conventions and rewriting the rules, options, and language that we use to

2   Larry Buchanan et al., "Black Lives Matter May Be the Largest Movement in U.S. History," *The New York Times*, July 3, 2020, https://www.nytimes.com/interactive/2020/07/03/us/george-floyd-protests-crowd-size.html.

3   Justin McCarthy and Steven Long, "Two in Three Americans Support Racial Justice Protests," Gallup, March 8, 2021, https://news.gallup.com/poll/316106/two-three-americans-support-racial-justice-protests.aspx.

express gender, just as they have changed the conversation around gun regulation and the dialogue on climate change. It's largely Zs who provide the vocabulary in which these debates are conducted.

Zs' mobilization on climate was initially inspired by Greta Thunberg in Sweden, who was only sixteen years old when she started her school strikes for climate change. Her fellow climate activists in the United States are equally young. On November 20, 2019, Generation We led the largest climate protest in history, mobilizing approximately 7.6 million people across 163 countries.[4]

These are highly visible, highly effective movements. But what do they mean? When we look back at this inflection point, how will we see the role of Zs in the trajectory of our shared humanity?

DIGITAL LIFE FORCE

Generation We have been connected to each other digitally since childhood. Many Zs weren't even born in 2007, when the iPhone first appeared; the oldest Zs were only ten. They can't remember a time without smartphones.

Older generations joke that smartphones are like another appendage for Zs. The observation has more than a grain of truth, but it doesn't have to be negative. Zs use their phones differently from previous generations. They don't just use them to do specific tasks such as texting or banking; they use them as

---

4   "7.6 Million People Demand Action after Week of Climate Strikes," Global
     Climate Strike, September 28, 2019, https://globalclimatestrike.
     net/7-million-people-demand-action-after-week-of-climate-strikes/.

a life force that connects them to the whole generation. That's one explanation for their relative unity—they're all linked.

The We Generation is the first generation that is mobile first. They don't even use computers unless they have to. For many adults, staring at a phone feels like being cut off from real life. For Zs, there's less distinction between their real-life community and their massive online communities. That level of connection is unique to Zs—it's what makes them such a power bloc and so collectively savvy.

And damn, they're *so* savvy. Their digital connections create an online generational epicenter where they access and share their diverse lived experiences and a whole global resource of knowledge. They learn about social problems and debate solutions; they build perspective and empathy via real stories of their peers, whether activists, entrepreneurs, or victims of oppression. And sometimes, they call each other out. They use those same digital platforms to gather support, organize, and mobilize action en masse.

In January 2021, it was largely Zs who led an online campaign to push up the share price of a moribund gaming retailer named GameStop in order to disrupt hedge funds and stockbrokers who had "shorted" the shares, counting on them to decline in value. Thousands of Zs drove GameStop's share price much higher than that of Apple. They realized that the coordinated actions of many thousands of individuals could shake a whole corner of the financial system.

The young disrupters exposed systemic flaws in the investment industry. It was a real flexing of Gen Z's muscles—and real evidence that one day, they really will be able to challenge the whole status quo.

GROWING INTO POWER

We see more evidence of the power of Generation We every day, and it's only going to increase. During the protests for racial equity and criminal justice reform in summer 2020, Gen Z mobilized to sabotage a Dallas Police Department (DPD) app that had been created to identify and arrest street protesters because they found the app prejudicial. Zs flooded the app with videos and photos, mostly of K-pop artists, crashing the site and forcing the DPD to abandon the initiative. That same month, Zs infamously foiled then-President Donald Trump's rally in Tulsa, Oklahoma, by reserving free tickets to the event in the thousands and artificially inflating attendance expectations, which turned out to be disappointingly small.

From the president to anyone in a position of power or responsibility, Zs aren't afraid to use new tactics to hold people accountable for their words and actions. They mobilize and disrupt companies, brands, and even award shows. They Twitter-bomb oil company executives seeking to drill in the wilderness. They chasten brands they feel pander to their generation.

They skewer powerful people for offensive, racist, sexist, and homophobic language and behavior—from both the present and the past. From the blackface photos of a prime minister to the racist tweets of *The Bachelor* contestants, sometimes it seems as if no one is immune.

This sort of action has become notorious as "cancel culture."

I hate that name, just as I hate the idea of preventing free speech. But I don't call it cancel culture. I call it accountability culture, which is how Generation We thinks of it. The purpose isn't to cancel people; it's to make people accountable for their words and behavior. It's to push public discourse and progress forward, as it has for #metoo and the racial justice movement.

It's about bold action.

It speaks to the immense power and savvy of Gen Z but also elicits fear and frustration among older generations who feel Zs wield it overzealously and without enough discernment.

That's a fair criticism. Most Zs agree cancel culture is overplayed and should be reserved for incidents that harm populations, not to quiet diverse perspectives. But it is important to understand that accountability culture has overwhelmingly positive intent, even if it has, at times, been an overly blunt weapon.

WHAT DO THEY WANT?

Many older Americans aren't sure what to make of the rapid rise of Generation We, from the school gates in Parkland to the steps of the US Capitol. Zs are outspoken and persistent, and happy to use unconventional tactics to disrupt the status quo. That makes people uncomfortable. No one knows where Zs are going to show up or what they're going to do. They're unpredictable.

They go beyond the usual channels past generations have used to articulate their voice—voting, signing petitions, writing to political representatives—because they've seen these actions alone don't produce the bold change they want.

To many people, it seems that Zs are just trying to tear everything down.

But to Zs, the issues we face are beyond politeness, so they are not asking politely. They're not quiet or meek. They are demanding. They are assertive and bold.

It sometimes feels as if the last couple of years have been an unbroken stream of youth protest, both online and in the streets.

It's like the teenagers are running the school. And everyone else is looking on and trying to figure out what that means, not just for today but for tomorrow. They can see the disruption and the energy, and they wonder where it's going to lead—or if it's going to lead anywhere. People have seen previous historical moments where fervor and enthusiasm have promised change, but no change has come. Remember the Arab Spring?

As I'll show you in this book, this time is already different.

WHY THEY MATTER

I've always been fascinated by culture and how it shapes people's attitudes and behaviors. When I was a kid, I devoured volumes of my parents' hardback *Encyclopedia Britannica*, skipping from country to country, reading about how people lived in each place, how they thought, and what they believed.

It's fitting that I went on to found a cultural consultancy, Global Mosaic, and have had the fortune to live on four continents and lead anthropological studies for companies, governments, and organizations across more than fifty countries.

Generations are like different countries. The formative experiences of each generation become the culture that cohort carries with them.

I've been studying generations for my entire career: first the boomers, then Gen X (that's me), and have shared the world's obsession with millennials for the past twentyish years. I find all of these generations fascinating in their own way, microcultures operating within and impacting our larger shared experience.

But here's the thing. For all of the expectations placed on the millennials—even their given name suggested they would leave a profound mark from the onset of this millennium—their impact has been incremental, not pivotal.

It turned out that 2000 was not really an inflection point. But 2020 *was*.

Gen Z is the first group of people I've studied who are part of a perfect storm, coming of age at such a pivotal time in history. The very foundations upon which we stand as Americans and global citizens are in the balance. We are in the process of reimagining our changing planet and how we live on it, enacting a new mandate for equity and racial justice, dismantling gender conventions, evolving to a less exploitative version of capitalism, and redefining the American dream as a more collective project.

As a postgraduate at the University of Chicago, I studied the historical drivers of sociocultural, economic, and political transitions and appreciate the larger historical perspective on the significance of this moment, early in the twenty-first century.

Gen Z didn't ask to be in this position, but this is where they are. This is where *we* are.

Generation We is going to be alive for this entire century, until 2100. They'll live through whatever happens with climate, whatever happens with race. They'll be enfolded in these issues from cradle to grave, whether they want to be or not.

They know this.

I founded ZSpeak as part of Global Mosaic to deeply engage with Zs across the United States and have been continuously collecting data on what they think, what they do, and what vision they have for our shared future. We've asked thousands of Zs how they feel about the issues facing them—and us. I felt compelled to write this book because I am in awe of their bold ideas. Their clarity of vision for what's possible. Their willingness to dismantle existing systems and rebuild them to work for the future. Their insistence on standing *together* to achieve broader-based equity for their cohorts marginalized by gender, race, or anything else. They hold strong ideals but are not idealists. They have already seen too much that is broken and hard and ugly in our world. This makes them realists. With real solutions. And this gives them fight.

There's a deeper story that needs to be told about Gen Z's impact that isn't getting heard through all the noise around their social media obsession, their cancel culture, and their angry street protests.

This book is about hopefulness at a time when our world sorely needs it. It's about the potential for positive impact and positive change. We're entering a revolutionary period, and I believe

Generation We will play a critical role in our evolution. Zs are young and imperfect and their methods raw. Transitions can be messy, but that's the work to be done and that's how progress gets made.

I think Gen Z are a reason for all of us to be optimistic about the future. In the first part of this book, I'm going to explain the *roots* of Zs' power, the conditions and characteristics that have made them such a force. In the second part, I'll share the extraordinary *transformation* they are poised to create in all of our lives: in gender, race, climate, capitalism, politics, education, and work.

I want to help you understand them so that you can understand more about what's coming. I also hope this book will make you a Gen Z ally. As we'll discuss later, there's a dark side to this generation, a price paid for growing up with all that connectivity and a front-row seat to the world's problems 24/7. Generation We needs our support, because at the moment they're carrying a disproportionate amount of the burden, at a stage in their lives when they should be studying, partying, traveling, meeting partners—almost anything other than mobilizing to try to ensure their own future.

Their story is important because it's *our* story. It's the story of how we can work together to craft our shared future.

Unity. Collaboration. Bold action.

Let's get to the work.

CHAPTER 1

The Most Pivotal Generation

"If we want to change the broken systems in our world, we must not be afraid to make big, disruptive changes. We have only a matter of years before we no longer have the chance to do anything about climate change, and people are dying every day because of police brutality. If we try to fix these issues through small incremental change, nothing will be achieved. We must tear down the old system before we build a new one—a functional society cannot be built on crumbling foundations."

—SIXTEEN-YEAR-OLD Z, MASSACHUSETTS

It's tempting to predict that Zs will follow the path of other generations. They start out young and feisty, reject the past, and rebel against their elders—until they inevitably go on to become part of the establishment.

It's tempting. But it's also mistaken.

For reasons I'll talk about, Generation We will be the most pivotal generation in recent history. Or the most impactful. Or the most disruptive. Whatever you want to call them, Zs will change the world in more profound ways than previous generations. The roots of their power are not only their size and digital savvy, but their unprecedented unity, relentless activism, radical inclusivity, and transformative creativity.

And these attributes are being unleashed during a period of disruption on all fronts: cultural, economic, environmental, political, social, and technological. The global pandemic alone made 2020 easily the most disruptive year since the onset of World War II.

THE GREAT DISRUPTORS

Generation We revel in disruption. Where older generations tend toward incremental change, Zs see disruption as being required to dismantle the systems no longer working in our world, whether in our energy systems or politics.

It will likely be unsettling and messy for some people much of the time and for everyone some of the time, but ultimately it will lead to progress.

Each generation works to redefine what came before them and thus to move society forward. But that progress comes in lurches and with missteps. It's not a linear path; it usually moves in small increments and often stalls, or even feels as if it's moving backward.

But social evolution, technology, and global connectedness have accelerated change so rapidly that generations are increasingly born into a world almost unrecognizable from the last.

Generations used to be defined in twenty- or twenty-five-year increments: the Greatest Generation, the Silent Generation, and the boomers. But Gen X, the millennials, Generation We—and the Alpha Generation that's up next—come in about fifteen-year increments, because social scientists recognize the rate of change as exponential. A teenager growing up just fifteen years ago wouldn't recognize much about growing up today; nor will a teenager growing up fifteen years in the future.

In this time of singular disruption, the shifts in a young person's life experiences are striking, even in fifteen-year increments. Gen X went to the mall and saved up for cassette tapes they listened to on a Walkman. Music was very precious, so kids were blissfully glued to MTV watching music videos. Remember "I want my MTV?" Meanwhile, the Berlin Wall was falling, the Soviet Union collapsed, and "the gays" were being blamed for AIDS, but for most of Gen X, all of that felt far away from their living rooms.

Jump fifteen years and millennial teens had iPods and access to digital music, which made music a little less precious because it could be easily downloaded and shared. Millennials still went to the mall and watched MTV, but the world was coming closer to home. The War on Terror reached the United States on 9/11. Major celebrities like Ellen DeGeneres were coming out, saying, "Yep, I'm gay," on the cover of *Time* magazine. And hundreds of thousands of people were clicking the Amazon "buy" button for the first time, worrying about credit card security and how Amazon kept its prices so low.

Another fifteen years, and a Z wouldn't recognize that world. A Z just touches or speaks to their devices to access anything they want: music, videos, information. They're as likely to buy goods online as to go to the mall. They don't watch much TV because they stream everything online. And they're completely exposed to everything happening in the world—for better and for worse. All the key issues are in play. The racial justice movement is at its first apex since the civil rights movement in the fifties and sixties. There's never been a similar gender revolution. It's the first time in a hundred years people have experienced a global pandemic.

Zs weren't naturally endowed with any great gifts that the millennials, Gen X, or boomers lacked. They're a product of their time and are coming of age during an era of unparalleled confluence of need plus ability.

WHAT MAKES A GENERATION?

As a social scientist, I've spent years studying sociocultural, economic, and political transitions. I'm interested in how society is constantly evolving. The evolution may not be linear or even logical, yet it steadily advances. People and generations are inherently diverse and complex, but generations are instructive in making us mindful of where we've come from and more intentional about our future.

Defining humans by generations is imperfect for many reasons. It's more of an art than a science. The parameters are usually set around defining or disruptive moments. Boomers, for example, are clearly defined because they started right after World War II in 1946 and extended until 1964, through the baby boom and the greatest economic boom in US history. Other generations might be determined by key advances or key shared experiences. Some generations are much more clearly defined and marked, while others are more amorphous.

All generations are equal, but some are more equal than others.

The Silent Generation, who were born between the World Wars, are very clearly defined. The boomers are well defined, too, coming from a period when the country was in an expansive frame of mind that translated to ambition, competition, and frankly, greed: *We're the biggest and the best, and we live in the best country.* That shared experience gave the boomers a dominant worldview, which is now regularly challenged via "OK boomer" memes.

My generation, Gen X, on the other hand, is poorly defined. Simply put, we're too young to be boomers and too old to be millennials. Even for Gen X, however, contemporary events impacted our attitudes and values, our behaviors, and our worldview.

A generation is a dynamic cohort. It evolves as its members go through life stages. We don't know exactly how the things that make Zs unique now will manifest as they age. We don't know what impact being the first digital natives will have on their ability to have successful interpersonal human relationships. We know they have a more open, flexible definition of gender, but we can't fully understand how that will impact their future partnering. We don't know which climate models they'll end up living with. Zs have spent part of their formative years in a pandemic cut off from school and friends. Again, no one has any idea how this will affect them.

FIVE GENERATIONS OF AMERICANS

There are five primary generations alive today, plus two very small ones.

Few of the Greatest Generation survive today. They were born before or during World War I, so any of them who are still living are now over ninety-five years of age.

The Silent Generation are seventy-five to ninety-five years old. They were born between the end of World War I and the end of World War II. They have traditional values that drove the country for a long time. But the Silent Generation were only 6 percent of the population in 2020, and their influence has waned as they've been replaced by younger generations.

BOOMERS

Boomers, born between 1946 and 1964, have held great economic and political influence for decades because of their size and the power and wealth they amassed during America's long postwar expansion. They have a strong work ethic allied to a very traditional definition of the American dream, which has largely shaped our approach to business, capitalism, competition, individual achievement, political dynamics, and "family values"—until now.

The boomers wanted to succeed as individuals. Their orientation was, "I'm going to work hard and be upwardly mobile, and I'm going to have a nice home, multiple cars, a beautiful family. I'm going to climb the career ladder, and I'm going to save for a good retirement." The economic boom they lived through made such ambitions feasible—for some. Many, many more missed out.

For Zs, boomers just don't get life in the twenty-first century. "OK, boomer" is essentially an acknowledgment that boomers lived through a bubble of privilege and economic abundance, creating systems that benefited them but drove inequality, division, and climate degradation on the other side.

It's a misperception that boomers were broadly involved in the liberation movements of the 1960s. Most boomers were only school-age during the civil rights movement, the Vietnam War protests, and the sexual revolution. The civil rights movement was mainly carried by the Black community. Most women didn't burn their bras. They just saw it on TV. The boomers are a far more conventional generation than many people imagine.

As we'll see in Part II of the book, many Z and millennial positions on issues are a direct backlash against boomer-built systems. The boomer construct is their push-off point, the status quo they seek to dismantle.

GENERATION X

Gen X was born from 1965 to 1980. They're the sandwich generation that has never gotten too much attention, the spam trapped between the more attractive boomers and millennials. They're the least clearly defined of the living generations, but they are interesting because they grew up while their boomer parents were on a huge economic and individualistic tear. Gen X were the original latchkey kids, our first foray into dual-working families and single-parent or stepparent households, because this was also the period when divorce became common.

The boomer economic tear ended in the energy crisis, economic downturns, corporate downsizing, and mergers and acquisitions. The Xs were the first generation raised knowing they may never do as well as their parents. Boomers had enjoyed an incredible ride, but Gen X was left thinking, "I guess I'll find my own way to school. I'll let myself in after school. Now my parents are divorced. That's okay, I'll make my own dinner. How am I going to get my first job during this economic crisis? My parents had it so easy and saved all this retirement money, and I just keep getting downsized."

In the fifties and sixties, it seemed that dinner was always on the table and *The Andy Griffith Show* was on TV. Then for Xs there wasn't even a parent home for dinner. Scandals like Watergate ushered in more skepticism and cynicism. One consequence is that Gen X are known for being very self-reliant and resourceful because they were not coddled. And we're known for being cynical because for most of our lives we've been told that everything was great until we came along too late to join the party.

Our parents lived in the world of *Leave It to Beaver*. We lived in the world of *Beavis and Butt-Head*. The bubble had burst.

MILLENNIALS

Millennials are the generation people know the most about. They're also the most instructive because, like Gen Z, they pivot off boomers.

Many observers lump millennials and Gen Z together, but that's an error. To most Gen Zs, millennials are really old. The oldest millennials are forty. Most of them are out of college and working, possibly married with kids, and possibly own their own homes. They're in the middle of what they call adulting. The two generations are dramatically different.

Millennials were born between 1981 and 1996. They've gotten a lot of attention because they eclipsed the boomers in size and came of age around the turn of the millennium to great fanfare and expectation.

Much has been written about millennials' upbringing and the "helicopter parenting" years: hands-on, scheduled parents eager to manage their kids' achievements so they could enjoy the reflected glory. Millennials were a Petri dish generation, put under the microscope not only by the parents who willed them to do well but also by society in general. They became a media staple. The press and TV were full of stories about "How will this affect the millennials?" or "What do the millennials think of this?"

Most were children during the eighties, a time of greater economic expansion and prosperity than the Xs, before another economic downturn followed in the nineties. That fueled an investment approach to parenting. The millennials were children of some of the younger boomers, who were all about managing and growing their assets—including their children.

Scarier things started to happen in the world for millennials. The first major school shooting happened at Columbine High School in Colorado in 1999; fifteen dead. Two years later was 9/11; 2,977 dead. We were told terrorism was on the rise. But because there were no smartphones or social media yet, parents sheltered millennials in a way Zs' parents cannot.

Kids of earlier generations swam in creeks, rode their bikes with no hands and without helmets, and disappeared under the bleachers. But this was the era of stranger danger and milk carton kids; the show *America's Most Wanted* launched. Millennials' parents wanted to shelter their babies from the evils of the world starting to encroach. Parents, teachers, and coaches protected millennials. Zs are the opposite. They have access to whatever is going on in the world. They've known since they were very young that bad stuff happens and that not everyone wins prizes.

The youngest millennials were only five when 9/11 happened, so a lot of them didn't understand it. There was a lot of guidance from the government, school boards, and even the media about how parents should talk to their kids about the attacks: what they should share and how they should present it. In contrast, Zs have been watching mass shootings unfold in real time, live-streamed to their phones, their whole lives.

The protected way millennials were raised has contributed to a bumpy adulthood for many of them. In some parts of the world, millennials are referred to as snowflakes because of their tendency to "melt" in the face of difficulty or discomfort (note "snowflake" has a different, political connotation in the United States). For sure, they entered a hire-and-fire workforce because the kind of capitalism that worked for boomers, with jobs for life and a steady income, had gone.

Millennials invented the term "adulting" to register their bemusement at having to do the things adults traditionally do: cleaning, cooking, going to the store, getting up on time, paying bills. The word appeared around 2008, and in 2016, it was the *Oxford English Dictionary*'s word of the year. It peaked when millennials started to move into their own condos and apartments. Previous generations had just stepped up to handle the responsibility of being an adult. Millennials bought T-shirts and pillows with slogans about how hard it was. The more hardened Zs enjoy ribbing the millennials for their relative softness and "adulting" challenges on TikTok.

GENERATION Z

Generation Z's birth years are roughly 1997 to 2010 or 2012 (it's still a little bit undefined). Like the boomers and millennials, they get attention for being a large generation, but even more so because they are driving a huge demographic and mindset shift. Due to their size and relative affluence, boomers have driven US political outcomes for a long time: as recently as 2000, boomers and older made up 68 percent of the voting electorate.[5] In the 2020 US presidential election, the oldest Zs made up 10 percent of eligible voters and, when combined with millennials, created a collective youth bloc of almost 40 percent, which matched the shrinking boomer and older cohort for the first time.[6] We've seen that Zs and millennials are very different, but they both tend to be more politically progressive than older generations. Even Z Republicans are more likely to say that government should do more and that Blacks are treated less fairly than Whites, and to attribute Earth's warming temperatures to human activity.[7]

If boomers had driven the election as they did until 2020, Donald Trump would have been reelected president.[8]

So the young generations are changing politics. They're also changing what the country looks like. In the 2020 election, for

5   Anthony Cilluffo and Richard Fry, "An Early Look at the 2020 Electorate," Pew Research Center's Social & Demographic Trends, Pew Research Center, January 30, 2019, https://www.pewresearch.org/social-trends/2019/01/30/an-early-look-at-the-2020-electorate-2/.

6   Ibid.

7   Kim Parker and Ruth Igielnik, "On the Cusp of Adulthood and Facing an Uncertain Future: What We Know about Gen Z So Far," Pew Research Center's Social & Demographic Trends, Pew Research Center, May 14, 2020, https://www.pewresearch.org/social-trends/2020/05/14/on-the-cusp-of-adulthood-and-facing-an-uncertain-future-what-we-know-about-gen-z-so-far-2/.

8   "Election Week 2020: Young People Increase Turnout, Lead Biden to Victory," CIRCLE at Tufts, November 25, 2020, https://circle.tufts.edu/latest-research/election-week-2020.

the first time, one-third of the electorate were non-White.[9] The boomers are 82 percent White,[10] so issues that uniquely affected BIPOC (Black, Indigenous, and people of color) never came to the fore in US politics. When millennials and Gen Z were asked what issues brought them to the polls in 2020, in contrast, their two main priorities were climate and racial equity.[11]

The one thing everyone knows about Zs, because the media bashes us over the head with it, is that they're the first digital natives. Gen Z never knew a time before smartphones and social media. Their median age was zero when Facebook launched in 2004, one when YouTube emerged a year later, two with the advent of Twitter, and three when Apple unveiled the first iPhone. The median Z was in kindergarten for the launch of Instagram and first grade when Snapchat was created.

Again, the technology is not the story. The story is who the technology has made them, the generation it created, what it allows them to do, and the role it allows them to take in the world.

They are the first generation with full awareness of the world and its problems. They're also the first generation to be digitally connected from a young age, and the platforms they use and the stories they share have created unprecedented empathy and

9   John Gramlich, "What the 2020 Electorate Looks like by Party, Race and Ethnicity, Age, Education and Religion." Pew Research Center, December 30, 2020, https://www.pewresearch.org/fact-tank/2020/10/26/what-the-2020-electorate-looks-like-by-party-race-and-ethnicity-age-education-and-religion/.

10 Richard Fry and Kim Parker, "'Post-Millennial' Generation on Track to Be Most Diverse, Best-Educated Generation Yet," Pew Research Center, August 14, 2020, https://www.pewresearch.org/social-trends/2018/11/15/early-benchmarks-show-post-millennials-on-track-to-be-most-diverse-best-educated-generation-yet/.

11 "Poll: Young People Believe They Can Lead Change in Unprecedented Election Cycle," CIRCLE at Tufts, June 30, 2020, https://circle.tufts.edu/latest-research/poll-young-people-believe-they-can-lead-change-unprecedented-election-cycle.

unity. Digital access has helped them develop a voice, so they are skilled at speaking out, with a larger voice than any previous generation. And the technology they can access has developed a whole generation of creators with remarkable imagination and ideas—including their own vision of what the country can and should look like in the future. Digital has made them the most technically savvy generation. They know how to organize and mobilize and how to create change in a way that no other generation has done.

So being the first digital natives is only important because it gives them unprecedented power—and they know how to use it. They were instrumental in keeping #blacklivesmatter going online; the phrase hash-tagged more than 26.8 million times in summer 2020. They mobilized to raise almost a million dollars for an Asian grandmother who fended off her attacker amid a rise in anti-Asian hate crimes in spring 2021. They also foiled a presidential rally.

This power can make them scary because it's never happened before. The kids are running the school, but they're savvy and informed and have purpose. It turns out they haven't just been watching TikTok videos and sending Snapchats. They use tech for fun, for sure, but they also use it with intent.

All this is what makes them so pivotal.

THE ALPHA GENERATION

With the Zs, we reach the end of the generational alphabet. Next comes the Greek alphabet, so we start with the Alpha Generation, which will probably be followed by the Betas (no one's quite sure yet).

The year divisions are unclear. Alphas will probably begin sometime between 2010 and 2012 and end sometime in the 2020s. They're a work in progress. Literally: 2.5 million Alphas are being born globally every week.[12]

As far as we can tell until now, the biggest formative event that will define the Alphas is the COVID pandemic (if a bigger global event happens during their formative years, then God help us all). The oldest are eight to ten years old, in elementary school or younger, so their childhoods will always be marked by COVID. They'll be the generation for whom school and work may forever be something that's more digital than IRL, or "in real life."

Whereas Zs grew up with iPhones and iPads, Alphas are growing up with voice commands and artificial intelligence. Their lives will be even more fused with tech. The implications of this level of technology and the effects of the pandemic will affect how human socialization and relationships look for a long time. It's ironic that the first US generation to experience a childhood pandemic in a century are likely to be the longest-living generation, thanks to general health advances. The majority of Alphas will celebrate the ringing in of the twenty-second century.

Their future stretches so far ahead that it's hard to predict much about it yet, but we do know that the Alphas will inherit whatever trajectory Gen Z creates. If Gen Z is opening up a world beyond gender, that's the world the Alphas will step into; if Gen Z opens up a creative economy, with an exponential range of possibilities for creativity and work, that's what Alphas will inherit; whatever steps Zs take to help the climate, that's the Earth the Alphas will walk on.

---

12   Alex Williams, "Meet Alpha: The Next 'Next Generation,'" *The New York Times*, September 19, 2015, https://www.nytimes.com/2015/09/19/fashion/meet-alpha-the-next-next-generation.html.

So whatever the future, the Zs will be pivotal.

CHAPTER 2

The Most United Generation

"Before TikTok, I only ever heard the experiences of those who go to my school or close friends in my area. Now I hear stories, experiences, and injustices told by people my age around the world. There's a bond you feel knowing you're all connected by one app."

—SIXTEEN-YEAR-OLD Z, MARYLAND

It's become a cliché that Zs have smartphones attached to their arms, and heads constantly buried in their screens. Just do a Google image search and every stock photo of Gen Z reinforces this.

Older generations mistakenly assume this means Zs barely know what's going on around them. But Generation We *does* know what's going on around them—and it's because of their phones.

Their phones are not just for Snapping and sharing memes. They are a portal into a vital generational epicenter that unites Zs regardless of whether they're urban or rural, red or blue state,

Black or White, Indigenous or immigrant, gay or straight, cis-gender or trans.

Unlike older generations, who use tech primarily to communicate with their IRL friends and family, Zs communicate with everyone everywhere. Zs thrive on absorbing and sharing a huge amount of information about lives very different from their own. About, for want of a better phrase, their shared humanity.

ONLINE UNITY

Lots of people have written about Zs and technology, but they focus on the data. They boil it down to figures: 74 percent of Gen Z spend their free time online; 55 percent use their smartphones five or more hours a day; Zs stream an average of twenty-three hours of video per week.[13] Although compelling, however, the data are not what's really interesting.

What's interesting is how this connectivity has shaped a generation that is united in a way previous generations can barely understand. It's like the movie *Avatar*, where a neural super brain connects all living things on the planet of Pandora, allowing the blue Na'vi people to plug in to a shared consciousness and a shared past, creating a huge organism far greater than the sum of its parts.

That's what's happening with Generation We. They've created a shared empathy by being connected and hearing each other's stories all the time in an intravenous process through their phones. Other generations didn't have that, even millennials.

---

13   Blake Morgan, "50 Stats All Marketers Must Know about Gen-Z," *Forbes*, February 28, 2020, https://www.forbes.com/sites/blakemorgan/2020/02/28/50-stats-all-marketers-must-know-about-gen-z/?sh=73c8899476do.

The median age of a millennial when the first iPhone came out was nineteen, and twenty-two when Instagram launched, though they are touted as the "Instagram generation."

Older generations celebrate the latest "tech toys," but for Zs, it's not about the hardware. Technology has always been there: it's the invisible enabler, and should be seamless. This is why Zs will not engage with an app or website that loads slowly. A Z's phone is less a physical device than an umbilical cord connecting them to their community 24/7.

It's sometimes said that Gen Z spends more time with their online communities than IRL. The truth is, Zs don't distinguish between them that rigidly. Z relationships move fluidly between digital and IRL. Anonymous AIM chat rooms are gone. Sites such as Reddit, Twitch, and Tumblr birth entire communities and relationships through uber-specific digital groups and interactive message boards where Zs connect and grow up alongside their online peers. Zs can take these digital friendships IRL through fan meet-ups, conventions, or gaming festivals like BlizzCon, which last netted 40,000 attendees in 2019.

THE CHOSEN APP

Many people first noticed the social media app TikTok when President Donald Trump announced his intention to ban it in August 2020. Most were probably bemused to learn that the government was taking on what was ostensibly a social media app full of silly videos aimed at kids. The US administration decided the Chinese-owned company was a national security risk, although it was also caught up in the fallout of an ongoing trade war between the United States and China.

Trump's executive order banning the company was eventually suspended by the courts on appeal—and the whole of Generation We breathed a sigh of relief.

So, too, should any Republicans seeking to attract young voters to the GOP, because shutting down TikTok is an action guaranteed to achieve exactly the opposite effect. Generation We loves TikTok. As of early 2021, TikTok had over 1 billion users in more than 150 countries and had been downloaded over 200 million times in the United States alone. The vast majority of Zs say TikTok is the app best suited to their generation (less than 20 percent said Snapchat or Instagram in contrast).[14]

The app originally allowed users to upload videos fifteen seconds long, then later extended that time limit to sixty seconds. To many older people, even millennials, this seems like a waste of time: dance trends, teenage vloggers, YouTubers pranking each other, K-pop fans. And there is a lot of that type of content.

But TikTok is also deadly serious—and hugely uniting. It's the We Generation's cultural heart.

TikTok is qualitatively different. That's why it's so popular and why it's so significant.

On social media platforms developed for millennials and older generations, like Instagram and Facebook, the user scrolls up and down the screen, and the feed shows the "friends" they follow and sponsored content that reinforces their views. It's insular and limited.

---

14   Research by ZSpeak by Global Mosaic, September 2020.

TikTok is inherently more inclusive. When Generation We opens TikTok, they land directly on their FYP (For You Page), which not only includes videos from their "friends" but also the latest videos trending anywhere in the world. Thanks to the algorithm, the more people who "like" a video, the more it will show up on other FYPs. And given Gen Z's dominance on the app, virtually all these videos are coming from other Zs. A video can spiral pretty quickly. TikTok user Christina Tinks posted a recommendation of her favorite water bottle that went viral with 5 million likes, despite being a nonsponsored, organic post. The water bottle sold out and immediately launched Tinks into a career as a full-time content creator. Similar stories happen every week.

Like most social media algorithms, a TikTok user's FYP will reflect past likes, so a more politically right-leaning Z will see more content/humor from other politically right users; someone who loves to read will see new book recommendations on their page and so on. However, TikTok's algorithm allows a more diverse range of content that transcends specific interests, so on any given day Zs around the world are seeing the same content. It might be a video audition for Lizzo's new reality show, focused on giving a platform to plus-sized models and dancers; or it might be a personal story of coping with depression during COVID, or an Asian youth's experience with a hate crime, or a call to buy fake tickets to a presidential rally.

Zs use TikTok to connect to their community and to the broader issues in the country and the world, curating the stories they find powerful to develop a shared consciousness and awareness.

Apps like TikTok create a far more united generation than the divided, riven, splintered nation of their elders. Although there are Zs across the political spectrum, in our research we don't find statistical differences in opinions on key issues by geography, as happens with older generations.

Zs are sharing the same videos—and everyone else isn't. What impacts their values, their worldview, their passions, and their interests doesn't only come from conversations around the dinner table or from the TV news, as it did for earlier generations. It comes largely from the pulsing 24/7 life force in their hand.

Gen Z's top three uses of TikTok are first entertainment (not surprisingly), but also news, and mobilizing and activism. About 25 percent of Zs use TikTok as their primary source of news[15] because—before their elders shake their heads with derision—they see it as a place for high-value discourse among a highly diverse universe of peers. Current events are told via firsthand stories of real people living the experiences without media spin. TikTok is as real and raw as Instagram is stylized and contrived, so it's the clear choice for Zs accustomed to seeing people taking to the streets, the planet burning, and mass shootings. They're not interested in the gloss; they want to know what's really going on.

On any given day, the trending fifteen-second shared videos might include a teenage girl's experience with fatphobia in a clothing store, a tour of a teenager's hometown in Svalbard (an island by the North Pole), a story time from a BIPOC youth on their experiences with police profiling, or a vlog-style walk along a Black Lives Matter protest in Chicago.

---

15   Research by ZSpeak by Global Mosaic, September 2020.

There are no filters and often no makeup. No airbrushed holiday beaches or food porn.

MORE CONNECTED THAN DIVIDED

Zs use the digital world to focus on their shared humanity. Generation We believes there is more that connects than divides them.

That's never been true before.

So a fifteen-year-old, no matter where they live, is likely trying to define themselves, as teenagers always have. Every day, they see stories of other fifteen-year-olds around the country, around the world, going through the same process. They can relate. Or perhaps they were born female and are comfortable with their identity as female, but they watch a video of someone their own age who is struggling to assert themselves as nonbinary or transgender. Again, they can sympathize because they're going through a similar identity exploration, even though they don't identify as trans. Or White kids can watch young BIPOC talking about their experience of racism or police brutality in America and feel deeply moved and affected by how personal their story is.

It's not the technology that unites Generation We. It's the stories. It's as though they all have access to everyone else's dinner tables and inner thoughts. One of the most popular video formats on TikTok are vlogs, which are like an open diary of one's day in video form. They were inspired by YouTube and the reality TV shows Zs grew up with, providing intimate, unscripted access to a person's life. They are highly diverse and specific to the creator: some vloggers document their day, what they eat, and what they wear, while others may share their struggles with anxiety or their journey on how to live a low-waste lifestyle.

Sharing stories shows Zs how similar they are, despite their different race or ethnicity, gender identity, sexual preference, or geography, in a way earlier generations have been unable to do. Ironically, the closest comparison to this Z experience is likely ancient times, when storytelling was a crucial form of social entertainment. Stories unite them and set a stage for omniculturalism. Zs are exposed to the lives and perspectives of many, many individuals, and that builds collective empathy.

When Zs talk, it's striking how much they use plural pronouns. They use *we* and *us* versus singular pronouns like *I* and *me*. A nineteen-year-old from Connecticut, for example, said, "Our current issues directly impact everyone and we need to work together to fix them."

It's rarely "I'm scared about our future, so I'm doing this." It's *everyone* is scared and *we* all need to work together. Constantly.

That feeling of interconnectedness and shared humanity was only reinforced by the COVID pandemic. Some 62 percent of Zs say they see people as more united than they were before COVID,[16] higher than any other generation. One fifteen-year-old in Iowa told us, "If there's anything we needed to learn from COVID, it showed us how much we really depend on each other as a species."

Plurals, again.

---

16   Research by ZSpeak by Global Mosaic, May 2020.

It's not that Zs are unaware of the divisions in our society. They can hardly avoid them after the last few years of politics. But they are also bolstered by evidence of citizens coming together to address a common goal. That's because they are inherently optimistic—even following a pandemic that disproportionately affected their schooling, their university experience, and their career opportunities.

Zs use the generational empathy created by social media story-telling to explain why they mobilize to support issues that don't directly affect them. Look at photos from Black Lives Matter protests in summer 2020, and you will see White kids (and every other race/ethnicity) standing with Black kids across the country. Some 88 percent of Zs feel Black Americans are treated differently from others and 83 percent feel the police use too much force. By June 2020, 77 percent of Zs surveyed had already attended a BLM protest and 62 percent said they were willing to get arrested during a peaceful protest to support Black equality.[17] That's collective action.

This generation is different. They're all involved in each other's struggles.

As we'll see, it's also worth noting that although Zs are so diverse, they're also the most inclusive generation. Generation We is projected to be the first non-White majority in US history. They also have far higher levels of gender nonconformity. No one is mainstream or "other," right or wrong, in or out.

---

17   Dominic-Madori Davis, "The Action Generation: How Gen Z Really Feels about Race, Equality, and Its Role in the Historic George Floyd Protests, Based on a Survey of 39,000 Young Americans," Business Insider, June 10, 2020, https://flipboard.com/article/the-action-generation-how-gen-z-really-feels-about-race-equality-and-its-role/f-9914927463%2Fbusinessinsider.com.

It seems paradoxical, but the diversity helps to create the unity.

So does the power. We've already seen how acting collectively makes Generation We so impactful, but they want older generations to join them. They want older people to show up at BLM protests. They want us to show up at their climate events. They want us to support their marches for gun regulation. They want us to use gender pronouns. They are pragmatists and they know older generations still hold much of the power to create the change they want to see.

(Of course, you might miss out if you're only on Facebook.)

Gen Z is sometimes called the iGen because of their digital nativism and hyperconnectivity. But it's not the connectivity that matters so much as the ability it gives them to show up and be impactful. That's why I call them Generation We. They're not only unique in terms of their mindset and how they organize but also in the disproportionate impact they can have on our larger community by forging a new era of more collective action at a pivotal time.

They're going to impact every aspect of society.

One reason Zs are so united in addressing issues that don't necessarily impact them directly is that they can see that most of the issues facing the world are collective crises.

They require collective solutions.

In times of crisis, collective action trumps individual action. On climate, for example, Gen Z are realistic about what they can achieve alone. A twenty-three-year-old from Arizona said, "The climate cannot be changed by one's individual actions alone but instead must be done by society as a whole. Changing what you eat and use can help but not nearly enough for substantial change. Right now, most of our problems come from large corporations prioritizing money over impact, and to fix climate change something must be done about that."

Generation We started acting collectively in 2018 with the shooting at Marjory Stoneman Douglas High School in Parkland, but once they saw the power of their activism, they got a taste for it. By now, many Zs have been coming together to march and to raise their voices as a united generation since they were in elementary school. The far majority of Gen Zs have participated in a march or a rally or a school walkout to date.[18] They often started at the age of ten or eleven, so they have had a taste of how collective power feels from a young age.

It's in their DNA.

COLLECTIVE DREAM

Generation We has a new definition of the American dream. In the past, the idea mainly gave individuals the license to act as they wanted or needed to ensure their pursuit of life, liberty, and happiness (or job, or home, or family). This was the American dream that saw the frontier pushed west by self-reliant pioneers; that saw immigrants arrive and make their fortunes; that saw kids leave anonymous midwestern communities and move west to become huge stars in Hollywood. It was based on the idea that anyone can achieve what they want to achieve through hard work.

18   Research by ZSpeak by Global Mosaic, May 2021.

For Generation We, that's a fallacy. They've grown up surrounded by fruitless striving and huge inequality. They can see that many BIPOC don't have equal access to the American dream. A child born in the inner city doesn't have equal access to the American dream. A recent immigrant doesn't have equal access to the American dream.

For Generation We, the American dream doesn't exist as long as huge swaths of the population are excluded by discrimination, systemic inequities, lack of opportunity, lack of education, or whatever else. They see a triumphant future as a collective project rather than an individual pursuit. They believe it can't be achieved for anyone unless it is achieved for everyone—not while so many people who are working so hard still lack access to the citizenship, education, work, or financial opportunity required to succeed. In the words of a nineteen-year-old from California: "I see the American dream as something that's only accessible to a small part of the population right now." A Z a couple of years older in Utah said, "The American dream is an idealized perspective that if you work hard enough, you can achieve anything. But this is a myth today, because privilege and circumstances are so varied and unequal."

Zs are reimagining the American dream, just as they are reimagining other aspects of our society (as we'll see). In their imagination, they seek to create a country in which all groups truly have equal access to opportunity and are no longer limited by their skin color, immigration status, gender, sexual orientation, or any other element of their self-identity.

It's a collective dream of a united nation.

But they're aware that it's only a dream.

It's going to be a constant theme throughout this book that Generation We are not idealists. They're realists. They know this stuff is easy to say and hard to achieve. But they're not saying it because they think these goals are easy to reach. They're saying it because their unity, diversity, inclusivity, and creativity make them bold enough to articulate big dreams and then try to figure out how to make them a reality.

And one of the ways to do this is through an app that most of their elders dismiss as worthless. As a sixteen-year-old from Illinois said, "TikTok provides a platform for Gen Z to talk about things we are passionate about and get our message across. It has united a whole generation together."

That's one of the major reasons the Zs are the most united generation. Now let's discover how that influences their role as the most activist generation.

CHAPTER 3

The Most Activist Generation

"It's important for my generation to have a voice right now because it's our future and the future of our children at stake. It's people my age that will have to deal with the repercussions in the future based on what happens now. Whatever we do now, all the decisions we make today, will have consequences in the future. The responsibility falls on our shoulders to pass on a future and planet where our kids have a chance to thrive."

—TWENTY-FOUR-YEAR-OLD Z, CALIFORNIA

Since 2018, one Z in particular has become one of the most famous people on the planet. It's difficult now to remember a time before the Swedish teenager Greta Thunberg became the voice of climate activism, but it's only been a relatively brief time since she started her Fridays for Future school strikes, during which she sat outside the Swedish parliament on her own with a handmade cardboard sign.

In the week of September 20, 2019, activists inspired by Greta organized the largest climate mobilization in history. An estimated 7.6 million people took part around the world.[19] It was organized by kids who had originally started following Greta's example by walking out of school on Fridays. In the United States, eight youth-led climate groups came together to form the US Youth Climate Strike Coalition, not only to organize these protests but also to articulate very specific goals and demands.

No one could fail to notice the September 2019 protest. The young protestors won widespread support. Companies like Patagonia, Lush, and Ben & Jerry's closed their businesses in solidarity, along with other institutions who heeded the call from kids to listen to the science. School systems closed down. The entire New York City public school system told students that no one had to show up at school that day.

Everyone was on the streets. It was clear that the kids wielded huge influence.

Generation We is inspired by ideals, but they're not a bunch of dreamers weeping over the fate of cute polar bear cubs.

On the contrary, they are highly pragmatic and solution-oriented. They understand the issues and underlying systems that need to be changed. They're not issuing vague demands like "Save the Whales," a staple of the 1970s. They have specific demands, such as keeping the temperature rise below 1.5°C.[20] Even the timing of the protest was strategic. The march was planned for three days before the United Nations Climate

19   "7.6 Million People Demand Action after Week of Climate Strikes," Global Climate Strike, September 28, 2019, https://globalclimatestrike. net/7-million-people-demand-action-after-week-of-climate-strikes/.

20   "Our Demands. Act Now!" Fridays for Future, May 2021, https://fridaysforfuture.org/ what-we-do/our-demands/.

Summit (COP 24). It was a message to world leaders to demand specific action to address climate change in a meaningful way. Organizers published five demands that they shared with the UN and government officials (including a Green New Deal).[21] It was a call to action from the youth of the world. Greta Thunberg and Jamie Margolin, (who was just fifteen when she co-founded the largest US-led youth climate organization, Zero Hour, in 2017) testified before US Congress two days before the strike and Greta delivered her scathing address to the United Nations three days later.

As they marched through the streets on September 20, Zs chanted, "We will make them hear us." They are desperate to be heard. In this aim, they employ lots of different means: old-school tactics like marching and chanting in the streets, as well as new-school tactics like organizing a seventy-two-hour livestream event for Earth Day 2020, which had more than 4.8 million views, or taking over celebrity social media accounts on key climate-related dates (such as those of Hailey Bieber, Jane Fonda, and Mark Ruffalo) to ensure their messages reached the celebrities' millions of followers.

Anything that will get them heard and help effect change.

At the time of the climate march, the median age of Zs was fifteen, so the majority were still in elementary, middle, or high school. At an age when earlier generations were walking to the park or to the mall, Zs are marching in the streets.

Civic participation is fused into their DNA from a young age.

---

21 "7.6 Million People Demand Action after Week of Climate Strikes," Global Climate Strike, September 28, 2019, https://globalclimatestrike. net/7-million-people-demand-action-after-week-of-climate-strikes/.

March for Our Lives, Climate Strike, BLM—it happens over and over again.

The last generation known for their activism was the boomers, but they did not organize as broadly, at such young ages, or in the same numbers. The largest antiwar protest in Washington, DC, during the Vietnam era was approximately 500,000 people in 1969.[22] That's a very small share of the large boomer population. Most boomers were just continuing to live their lives. They read about the protests or saw them on TV, but they weren't really engaged. And the demands of those who did show up in DC weren't as sophisticated: End the War; Bring Our Boys Home.

In contrast, the most activist generation knows exactly what they want. They are coming of age at a pivotal time as critical issues reach an apex—the climate crisis, lack of response to gun violence, state-sanctioned violence against their Black peers—and their tech savvy allows them to engage and organize on a highly sophisticated level. They are already changing the trajectory on the most critical issues of our time.

The climate strike on September 20, 2019, has continued to drive climate momentum across the world, including gains for Green parties in Europe and climate organization-led voter drives in the United States in November 2020 that resulted in a "climate mandate" for the Biden administration. The change in public sentiment was reflected in Biden's decision to rejoin the Paris Climate Accords by executive order within hours of becoming president in January 2021, and his ambitious climate plans, which are on an unprecedented scale.

---

22 Erin Skarda, "Top 10 Most Influential Protests," *Time*, June 28, 2011.

TIME FOR REPAIR

Zs are the generation that can help us mend our broken systems at this pivotal time.

Generation We grew up during a period of great instability in so many areas: culturally, economically, environmentally, politically, socially, and technologically. Rarely has there been so much change in such a short time. There has been no constancy, just constant adaptation.

Older generations have talked about climate change for a while, but Generation We was born in a climate that is already in crisis. They were born onto a planet that is already hotter than it should be. Constant natural disasters are part of their news cycle: record-setting droughts, record-setting floods, record-setting hurricanes, record-setting wildfire seasons. The six years from 2015 to 2020 were the hottest on record.[23] Zs' science classes revolved around climate as early as kindergarten and progressed to climate models and projections on melting ice caps, rising sea levels, and natural disasters by elementary school. Quite the departure from my childhood picking up neighborhood trash and making papier-mâché globes.

Zs have also grown up in a post-9/11 world, where active terrorism remains a constant possibility. They grew up with metal detectors. They've practiced active shooter drills since elementary school, just as students used to practice tornado and fire drills.

Then there's the economic instability. The recession of 2008

---

23   Katherine Brown, "2020 Tied for Warmest Year on Record, NASA Analysis Shows," NASA, January 14, 2021, https://www.nasa.gov/press-release/2020-tied-for-warmest-year-on-record-nasa-analysis-shows.

and 2009 brought with it the worst employment rates since the Great Depression in the 1930s. It added to corporate instability and job instability. A similar growth in unemployment and economic instability occurred during the COVID pandemic of 2020. Unlike the millennials, who grew up with parents who felt financially secure, Zs grew up with parents stressed by the lack of financial security.

That's one reason Gen Z is quite conservative in spending and investing. They're like the generation that came out of the Great Depression.[24]

Financial inequality is another crisis. It's been rising since 1980, but during Zs' lifetimes it has been on a tear.[25] Financial inequality has increased every year since they've been born, and the gap has widened. Other generations have lived through times of inequality, but inequality in the United States today has reached an unsustainable level. The inequities are more visible than ever. Generation We walk around their cities or their towns, and it's all so clear: they notice the increase in homeless people and the lines for food assistance; they see their fellow students stretching themselves thin working two or three jobs to support increasing college tuition rates. It's just part of their reality.

Zs came of age during a time of great political divisiveness, particularly during the Trump presidency from 2016 through 2021. Think of all the debates they've lived through, centered on which populations deserve which rights. Do gay people deserve

24 Amy Lynch, "Gen Z Kids Are Like Their Great-Grandparents. Here's Why," Generational Edge, July 8, 2015, http://www.generationaledge.com/blog/posts/genz-like-grandparents.

25 Juliana Menasce Horowitz, Ruth Igielnik, and Rakesh Kochhar, "Trends in Income and Wealth Inequality," Pew Research Center, August 17, 2020, https://www.pewresearch.org/social-trends/2020/01/09/trends-in-income-and-wealth-inequality/.

the right to be married? Who has the right to control wom-en's healthcare? Do we separate immigrant children from their parents? Should the police be abolished? Which populations deserve the right to vote? These types of cultural debates have dominated their dinner tables and classrooms most of their lives.

Although issues like climate, gun regulation, gender, and racial equity have broad support across the generation, Zs also mobi-lize as passionately on more partisan issues in smaller subsets, such as the country's largest annual anti-abortion rally, March for Life, in DC, which drew a crowd of around 100,000 people in 2020 and has a lot of digital support on apps like TikTok.

THE GEN Z BURDEN

When it comes to campaigning, Zs don't reject traditional meth-ods. But they believe that they need to use all tools at their disposal. As twenty-three-year-old voting rights activist Evan Malbrough from Georgia explained, "You can't build a house with just a hammer."

For Zs, that means the system isn't changed by voting alone. Sure, much as the hammer is critical, so is voting. But Zs know their goals require changes in thinking and change from inside some of our fundamental systems, which means raising the deci-bel level. The goals of their in-your-face protests and online tactics are not simply to get their voices heard but also to chal-lenge us to look critically at the systems in place and how to improve them.

Gen Z's engagement showed up in the 2020 election when an unprecedented number of youth voted. Between 52 and 55 percent of eighteen- to twenty-nine-year-olds voted in the presidential election.[26] In the past, that figure was as low as 25 percent. This younger cohort—a combination of Zs and millennials—made up 17 percent of the popular vote in 2020.[27] That means almost one in five people who voted were in their teens or twenties.

So Zs understand the importance of voting, clearly.

But Zs acknowledge that not all issues can be solved through ballots in boxes, especially with the rise of voter suppression laws in their lifetime. Along with getting out the vote, 86 percent of Zs believe that large-scale peaceful protests and political demonstrations are necessary to create a significant change.[28] They've also been educated on 1960s civil rights sit-ins and planned mass arrests and 1980s AIDS die-ins and public mass memorials. They know sometimes you have to be loud to be taken seriously. Forty-three percent of Zs agree that protests have to be violent in order to create change, but the majority said they should use any means of peaceful protest at their disposal.[29]

Twenty-one Gen Zs are suing the US government for violating their constitutional rights to life, liberty, and prosperity by failing to protect essential public resources. In other words, the government wasn't protecting the environment or the planet.

---

26 "Election Week 2020: Young People Increase Turnout, Lead Biden to Victory," CIRCLE at Tufts, November 25, 2020, https://circle.tufts.edu/latest-research/election-week-2020.

27 John Gramlich, "What the 2020 Electorate Looks Like by Party, Race and Ethnicity, Age, Education and Religion," Pew Research Center, December 30, 2020, https://www.pewresearch.org/fact-tank/2020/10/26/what-the-2020-electorate-looks-like-by-party-race-and-ethnicity-age-education-and-religion/.

28 Dominic-Madori Davis, "The Action Generation: How Gen Z Really Feels about Race, Equality, and Its Role in the Historic George Floyd Protests, Based on a Survey of 39,000 Young Americans," Business Insider, June 10, 2020, https://www.businessinsider.com/how-gen-z-feels-about-george-floyd-protests-2020-6.

29 Ibid.

Any tactics that will work.

Having grown up with instability and culture collision, Zs then lived through an unprecedented global health crisis with the COVID pandemic. They attended elementary school, high school, and college remotely and were isolated from their friends. Their extracurriculars, proms, graduations, and job offers were canceled. The pandemic interrupted so many rites of passage that every generation before them in recent memory has enjoyed. Many Zs missed these formative moments, and they're a product of that fact.

Not since the Silent Generation, born between the wars, grew up during World War II has any other generation grown up with so much instability, disruption, or lack of constancy.

And none of this has just been a backdrop for Zs. They have witnessed it all, with unfettered digital access that puts all of this inequity, strife, conflict, and uncertainty front and center in their lives. When 9/11 happened, millennial kids didn't have phones. Perhaps their parents told them about it at the dinner table, or perhaps they didn't. It was different for Gen Z. From their lunchrooms, from their practice fields, from their bedrooms late at night, they watch the aftermath of shootings, the aftermath of hurricanes, the plight of migrants at the borders. They watch incidents of police brutality unfolding in real time from wherever they are.

Those places that have always been associated with innocence— the school lunchroom, the soccer field, the bedroom—are constantly invaded by the reality of the world.

This has made Zs grow up really fast. It's stolen their childhoods. It has placed a huge weight on them. I call it the Gen Z burden.

We asked Zs at what age they were awoken to activism or social engagement by some event or another. Over half—56 percent—were twelve or younger. And a third—37 percent—said they were nine or younger.[30] One remembered: "I was in fourth grade when California proposed Proposition 8, which would take away the right to same-sex marriage. As a fourth grader, I saw signs around the neighborhood that read: *Say Yes to Proposition 8.* I thought that seemed really unfair. And it was the moment in my life when I began to understand inequality."

A nineteen-year-old from Georgia talked about the 2012 movie theater shooting at the premiere of *The Dark Knight Rises* in Aurora, Colorado. He said, "My dad, my brother, and I went to see that movie that same night that it came out. And it's crazy to imagine that that could have been us."

To Zs, it feels like they are part of the story. They're trapped inside it. Everyone's a player, whether they want to be or not.

A fourth of Zs are Latinx (a recently coined gender-neutral term for a person of Latin American origin or descent), so immigration raids and deportations are immediate for them. They and their communities are vulnerable. Almost half of Zs are non-White, which is why violence against Asian Americans, the struggles of Indigenous people to ensure their access to clean air and water, and the continuous fight for a fairer criminal justice system are personal, too. They feel like participants more than observers.

When Zs were asked how they felt about the current state of the world, only 7 percent said they were happy. Over a third (36

---

30   Research by ZSpeak by Global Mosaic, May 2020.

percent) said they were sad or disappointed, 23 percent said they were anxious or worried, 10 percent embarrassed, and 8 percent angry (the rest were unsure how to answer).[31]

But 85 percent of Zs said that they were optimistic that we could work toward a better future.[32]

It makes sense, given what they've been exposed to, that Zs are sad, disappointed, anxious, worried, embarrassed, and angry. Yet they also have an inherent optimism. Whether they're more optimistic than previous generations of youth, we can't say. But we *can* say that they're remarkably optimistic and resilient.

STAYING RESILIENT

A lot of Zs' resilience comes from their activism. They've been making an impact since 2018 and, in that time, have learned how to connect with and support each other, as well as how to organize together. It's circular. They see the impact they can have and how they can influence change, and that fuels their optimism that they can change things even more.

This optimism and resilience serves them well. Older generations grew up watching Saturday morning cartoons and MTV and obsessing over music videos. But for Zs, even though they're consuming funny videos on TikTok, they're also consuming unedited, undiluted footage of what's happening in the world. That's the context for everything they do, and it inspires their activism.

---

31 Research by ZSpeak by Global Mosaic, May 2021.

32 Ibid.

Activism is a constant element in and inherent part of their lives in a way it never has been for earlier generations. When we asked 1,500 Zs across the country how important it was for them to personally speak out and have a voice on issues happening in the community, country or world, every single one said that it was important or really important.[33] None of them said, "I can't be bothered" or "I'm not that political." None of them wanted to leave it to a few activists. One hundred percent wanted their own say.

And not just on social media. These issues expand into every aspect of Zs' lives. Of course they discuss them online, but 82 percent said they also discuss political and social issues with their friends in person.[34] That's right: today's teenagers hang out and talk about social issues. Seventy-seven percent of respondents said they have these discussions at home with their families, and 76 percent said they have them in the classroom.[35]

In the past, classrooms were usually about the textbooks. Now they're about current events, redefining the American South's relationship to Confederate iconography or debating whether the electoral college is still relevant in our modern political system. These types of topics were once untouchable. Now they're in every aspect of life.

Social media gives Zs a public platform for their voice from an extremely young age. The average Gen Z creates their first social media account by middle school (if not earlier). From that point on, they're pushing out content, filming videos on TikTok,

---

33 Research by ZSpeak by Global Mosaic, May 2020.

34 Ibid.

35 Ibid.

posting pictures on Instagram. It's not unusual for a tween to post something on TikTok or YouTube and get thousands of likes. Older Americans who post something on Facebook get dozens or a few hundred views from their community. They use it as a private, personal platform. But Zs posts are truly public. They have a comfort level with having a public voice and putting content out there from a very young age. It feels natural to them. They have no hesitation about being on a public stage. As we'll see when we discuss the Most Creative Generation, they love to create content. Older generations, even millennials, are mostly content consumers. Gen Z are content creators. They set out to get followers and likes. It's a widespread goal to become a creator or influencer on TikTok or YouTube.

It's important to note Zs are simultaneously savvy about internet privacy laws and the ways that many social media apps like Instagram record conversations and eye movements in order to target users with specific advertisements.

Still, Zs want more people to see their stuff. They feel they're being called to this moment and have been given an imperative to lead. They see it as an obligation and a responsibility. One seventeen-year-old from Colorado said, "If we don't speak out, change will not happen. Change only comes when light is shed on the subject. With more people speaking, the more important it becomes. If we speak loud enough, higher authorities can't ignore us." And an older Z in Ohio echoed the sentiment: "If we aren't speaking out for truth and justice, we're letting lies and injustice win. Silence is action as much as words, so we should choose words."

Generation We feels that the issues they face are the accumulation of things that have not been addressed by previous generations. If older generations haven't made progress, they aren't going to sit around and allow the same cycle to continue perpetuating itself.

How many years have boomers had to sort things out? How about Gen X? It turns out that millennials have had little influence on determining the direction of the century so far, even though they came of age as it began. It's Zs who will do that. And they will tell you openly how previous generations have let them down.

Generation We believes they have to lead because there's no time to waste. Time is a luxury we don't have when the planet is dying, when kids are being shot in school, when Black people are being shot in the street, when mobs are storming the Capitol. As a nineteen-year-old Z from Massachusetts told me, "Everything that we're having to address is the accumulation of issues that previous generations didn't address. And our generation is going to stop it. It's going to stop at our doorstep. We're not going to kick the can down the road to the next generation. There isn't time. It's landed on us. We need to fix it."

This is why activism is more personal for Zs than for other generations. It matters more to them, in the same way the outbreak of a war matters more to the young people liable to get drafted to the front lines.

Current climate models from the IPCC (UN Intergovernmental Panel on Climate Change) project that if we stay on our current trajectory, Earth's temperature could reach 1.5°C over preindustrial levels (a marker for increased ecological/social instability) as early as 2030.[36] When older generations look at stats and

36 IPCC, "2018: Summary for Policymakers," in *Global Warming of 1.5°C* (Geneva: World
    Meteorological Organization, 2019).

projections like this, we see abstract lines on a graph. Zs, on the other hand, might see the year they are meant to graduate from college.

That makes it personal.

It's also more personal when Zs are the ones who are locked into classrooms during active shooter drills. It's more personal because half of them are BIPOC, so maybe they or their friends have been pulled over by the police for minor infractions because of the color of their skin. They have been taught how to put their hands on the dashboard to help keep them safe. Zs live these things. And as far as immigration goes, with a quarter of the Z population identifying as Latinx, some may have had family members deported or have had to stay home because they're afraid of immigration raids.

Generation We weren't born to do this. They're just normal kids who were born into a specific moment in time. When Zero Hour started, a couple of fifteen-year-olds thought they wanted to do something so they started to organize their friends. Now they're the largest youth-led climate organization in the United States—and they're all still kids. Most are high schoolers, though a couple are in college. They go to school by day and are on conference calls or board meetings in the evenings. They were just people in a certain place at a certain time.

Greta Thunberg is an anomaly. She acquired a remarkable amount of knowledge about the environment. Other kids, like Emma Gonzales and David Hogg from the Parkland shooting, just happened to be in the wrong place at the wrong time. Emma was involved in school theater, so she was good at speaking in public. A shooting happened to take place at her school, and she happened to take the microphone—and her life was changed forever. She wasn't planning to be an activist.

The same with Mari Copeny, who was only eight when she wrote an open letter to President Obama in 2016, challenging him to visit her hometown of Flint, Michigan, because the water was contaminated with lead and thus undrinkable. She explained the particular effects this would have on children who had to drink the water. Her letter was published by the *Los Angeles Times* and made the national news, while Mari went on to meet Barack Obama, Hillary Clinton, and Donald Trump to discuss the issue. In an instant, she was transformed from being an advocate for her community to campaigning against environmentalism and racism across the country, recognizing that environmental problems often have a disproportionate impact on BIPOC communities. She founded local community organizations that raise thousands of dollars for clean drinking water for kids and also for school supplies. At age thirteen, with her own activist website, Mari declared her intention to one day become president.

Mari originally took action only because her community was in crisis and not enough was being done. That's a frustration widely felt by Zs. As a twenty-year-old from Texas observed, "If we don't speak up, who will? We cannot wait and pass on the responsibility to someone else. It takes a collective unity of the people to make a difference and dismantle the broken systems of power which exploit people."

You can see all this activism mindset reflected in Zs' role models. For older generations, role models were often movie stars or professional athletes, people who were doing "cool" stuff. Zs tend to choose role models who are making the world a better place. They love Alexandria Ocasio-Cortez, for example. If they talk about movie stars, it's stars who are using their position to make a positive impact, like Lizzo's body positivity movement, Harry Styles marching in BLM protests, Shailene Woodley being arrested at the Dakota Access Pipeline, or Leonardo DiCaprio and his climate advocacy. A twenty-one-year-old in Kentucky told me, "When I was younger, I looked up to Leonardo DiCaprio for his acting. But when I followed him on Instagram, it wasn't pictures of his life but things going on with the environment. Without him and the issues he shares, I'd have no clue they existed. I'd be in the dark about a lot of problems with the destruction of the environment. And I feel so strongly about protecting our planet now because of him."

The majority of the role models Zs note come from their own generation, like Greta, Jamie, and Mari, or Emma Gonzales and David Hogg. People much like themselves who are making a positive impact on the world.

PRIVILEGE AND INTERSECTIONALITY

There's been a lot of talk in the last couple of years about privilege, particularly White privilege and male privilege.

Gen Zs are the generation that is really internalizing what this means. One nineteen-year-old from Massachusetts said, "As a woman, I know systemic injustice, but as a White woman, I have enough privilege to be able to stand up and speak. Not only for myself but for others who are not able to speak."

Zs are highly aware of how their privilege gives them both the responsibility and an amplified voice to speak out for people who don't have as much influence. Generation We work together to address injustices, even if they don't impact them personally. Only 14 percent of Gen Zs are Black, but 90 percent of Zs support Black Lives Matter.[37] Although 16 percent of Gen Zs identify as LGBTQ+,[38] 88 percent support equal rights for people who identify as LGBTQ+.[39]

Previous generations lived in geo-fenced privilege. They weren't exposed to all of the different stories and diversity on their social media feeds the way Zs have been.

When I grew up in a predominantly White neighborhood and went to a predominantly White school and a predominantly White college, I wasn't aware of my privilege. I was geo-fenced.

That's impossible for Zs. Digital experience makes them hyper-aware of how different people have different access or are treated differently. They're the first generation to really see and actively understand the privilege they have.

You can't fix something if you can't see it. So if you're not aware of systemic racism, you're not going to feel it's such a problem; but if you are *aware* of systemic racism and you acknowledge it, that's the first step to becoming an ally. Generation We can see what previous generations didn't see—and many still don't.

Intersectionality—the idea that all issues intersect—is another buzzword and key idea for Generation We. For example, to talk

---

37 Dominic-Madori Davis, "The Action Generation: How Gen Z Really Feels about Race, Equality, and Its Role in the Historic George Floyd Protests, Based on a Survey of 39,000 Young Americans," Business Insider, June 10, 2020, https://www.businessinsider.com/how-gen-z-feels-about-george-floyd-protests-2020-6.

38 Jeffrey M Jones, "LGBT Identification Rises to 5.6% in Latest US Estimate," Gallup, April 3, 2021, https://news.gallup.com/poll/329708/lgbt-identification-rises-latest-estimate.aspx.

39 Research by ZSpeak by Global Mosaic, May 2021.

about climate, one also has to acknowledge that BIPOC, front-line, lower socioeconomic communities, and poorer countries will be disproportionately affected by climate change.

Previous generations tended to focus on one issue: this organization focused on racism, this one on sexism, and so on. Z organizations tend to address things at their intersection. They believe you can't address one issue without addressing others. To return to Zero Hour, the youth-led climate group, they describe themselves as a climate and environmental justice organization that works at the intersection of equity, race, and economic justice.

They want to address the root causes of climate change, which they identify as extractive capitalism, colonialism, racism, and sexism. They focus on people on the front line in marginalized communities, because climate change will affect those populations disproportionately. They want to transition from a fossil fuel industry to a renewable energy economy, but they understand the complexities. They know they need to create equity for populations at the margins, which includes many people who work in the fossil fuel industry, mines, or refineries.

Zs are oriented toward action. They believe that older generations talk a lot but don't do very much. The activism of the sixties was relatively limited, and for the half century since, there's been little. Zs are naturally doers and risk takers. They're not afraid to try to achieve change, especially if they can see that the consequence of not changing is riskier. More than half of Zs say that climate change has already impacted where they live.[40] Climate denial isn't even up for debate. The facts are clear.

---

40   Research by ZSpeak by Global Mosaic, May 2021.

The consequence of not acting seems higher than the consequence of acting.

We asked Zs what they thought the world would look like in 2050, given our current climate trajectory. They described a nightmare by Bosch. Many places in the world will become uninhabitable. Other areas will explode with population density. There'll be conflicts resulting from diminishing resources, and dramatic increases in economic inequity. The pictures Zs paint of what our world will look like if we don't do anything about the climate are terrifying.

The consequence of not acting is riskier than any action.

ACCOUNTABILITY CULTURE

There's a lot of debate about cancel culture. As I've said already, I don't think Generation We is trying to cancel people and certainly not to hurt people. Rather, they're trying to create a culture and system of accountability. They believe that unless people are made accountable, there can be no change to the systemic problems within big corporations or government.

Generation We is trying to get right to the heart of who needs to accept accountability in order to usher in change. They feel patronized when they are told to recycle their trash in the lunchroom, while corporations are allowed to burn fossil fuels with impunity.

They take it personally, so they're always going to call it out.

Zs are solution-oriented. They have sophisticated goals, like the five demands they made at the Climate Strike, directed at the politicians and officials at the UN Climate Summit. They have real, tangible goals.

One way they make an impact is through what they buy. We'll talk about Conscious Capitalism more in Part II, but for now, know that how Zs spend their money is part of their activism. It's a way they can make a positive impact on the things they care about. Zs make informed purchases based on a company's environmental behavior, social actions, and core values.

For many Zs, day-to-day life is an act of activism. Even when they are just scrolling online, their choices are determined by an underlying set of principles that they wish to bring change. The ads they watch, the food they eat, the clothes they wear— every decision is imbued with consciousness. Every decision is a choice that impacts the planet. Every choice supports progress—or the status quo.

As we'll see, these decisions, multiplied by millions, bring change.

Zs are not disgruntled youth just lamenting the failure of older generations, or idealistic children fixated on niche causes. Digital access has given them an awareness and sophisticated understanding of the problems facing the world today and the underlying systems that need to change. They are about collective action, and they will create—and already have created, for that matter—a formidable power bloc despite their youth.

Zs don't see movements like Black Lives Matter as an event or a moment in time. They see them as an ongoing imperative because systemic racism needs to be addressed.

Generation We's activism is going nowhere. We're going to keep seeing them in the streets. They'll keep flexing their muscles. But there's one thing to bear in mind, as we're about to see in the next chapter: these protests are not meant to exclude the rest of us. In fact, Generation We wants to include everyone.

CHAPTER 4

The Most Inclusive Generation

"Our generation is the least racist, the least sexist, the least likely to judge someone because of sexuality or circumstance."

—THIRTEEN-YEAR-OLD Z, NEW JERSEY

In the aftermath of the 2020 presidential election, there was much celebration about the election of Kamala Harris—who is, all at once, the country's first female, Black, and South Asian vice-president—and what it said about the country's progress toward representation.

Not for Generation We, though. For them, this particular narrative was not an achievement to be celebrated. It should be a given. Zs have already had a Black president for half their lives. They're far less interested in celebrating achievements than in disrupting the systemic forces that still prevent racial and gender equity.

A SKIRT FOR PROM

Generation We is the most racially diverse generation in US history—and the first projected not to have a White majority. Zs are also far more likely than older Americans to reject the binary gender labels of male and female.

Generation We prefers to see each other as individuals, regardless of external characteristics of biology or race. It's this view that allows them to go beyond the markers they believe limited previous generations.

Take Jaden Smith. If at all, older Americans are aware of him as the offspring of celebrity couple Will Smith and Jada Pinkett Smith, or as an actor in his own right. For Zs, however, Smith is someone disrupting the traditionally gendered fashion space. He is a leading spokesperson for inclusivity and expressivity, two of the defining characteristics of Generation We.

In his teens, Smith—who was born in 1998, putting him among the oldest Zs—began to challenge who can wear what clothing by wearing a white skirt and black tux to prom, a flowered dress to Coachella, and famously modeling a skirt for Louis Vuitton in 2016. He's gone on to found his own clothing line, MSFTSrep—a play on the word *misfits*—with the goal of creating not just a fashion brand but a community that welcomes everyone and every form of self-expression. Smith explained, "I'm taking the brunt of it so that later on, my kids and the next generation of kids will all think that certain things are normal that weren't expected before my time."

Zs like Smith are challenging traditional gender conventions. They are also redefining ideas about inclusivity and exclusion by rejecting labels in favor of individual self-expression. Generation

We is the most inclusive generation partly *because* it's also the most expressive generation. They believe individuals should be free to dress and behave as they like, regardless of their sex assigned at birth. No human should be limited by biology, skin color, nationality, or any other qualities they happened to show up on the planet with.

Zs' recalibration of ideas around race and gender are inherently inclusive (like Smith's brand) and reject the concept of "us" versus "them" or any population being the "other," both of which have shaped US history dating back to the arrival of the first Europeans. As we'll discuss in Chapter 7, these are huge changes that will lead to a new type of inclusivity and an era of acceptance and collaboration.

THE NEW MATH OF INCLUSIVITY

The scale of the momentous change Generation We will bring can be expressed as two simple fractions: one-half and one-third.

Currently, only 52 percent of Gen Zs are White.[41] According to the US Census Bureau, that tiny majority will tip the other way by 2026 thanks to continued immigration, mainly by Latinx. One-half refers to the number of Zs that will be non-White.

One-third refers to the number of Zs who identify as being nonbinary, meaning they do not conform to the traditional definition of being a "male" or a "female" but somewhere along the spectrum.[42]

---

41   Kim Parker and Ruth Igielnik, "What We Know about Gen Z So Far," Pew Research Center, February 9, 2021, https://www.pewresearch.org/social-trends/2020/05/14/on-the-cusp-of-adulthood-and-facing-an-uncertain-future-what-we-know-about-gen-z-so-far-2/.

42   Research by ZSpeak by Global Mosaic, July 2020.

One-half and one-third. The new math of inclusivity reflects demographic change, which is impacting racial and ethnic diversity, and culture change, which is impacting gender identity.

Generation We are the most racially and ethnically diverse generation since the founding of the country. For nearly 250 years, the United States has operated with a White majority, with everyone else reduced to the minority. Within Generation Z, these numbers will be overturned for the first time, with a population that is fully 25 percent Latinx, 14 percent Black, 6 percent Asian, and a growing percentage of other and multiracial identities.

For context, boomers are 18 percent non-White, Generation X are 30 percent non-White, and even the millennials are only 39 percent non-White.[43]

If a Z grew up in a large US city, two-thirds of their cohort are already non-White, with White Zs in the minority. In many parts of the Southwest, Latinx represent 40 percent of the Gen Z population.[44]

Of course, racial balance varies widely from region to region, city to city, even from block to block. Largely due to continued segregation, a Z in inner-city Chicago may go to school with mainly Black teenagers, while in a far suburb have almost solely White classmates. Geographical division is real, though Z online spaces bring them together, defying zip code limitations.

---

43 Kim Parker and Ruth Igielnik, "What We Know about Gen Z So Far," Pew Research Center, February 9, 2021, https://www.pewresearch.org/social-trends/2020/05/14/on-the-cusp-of-adulthood-and-facing-an-uncertain-future-what-we-know-about-gen-z-so-far-2/.

44 Ibid.

We know that changing demographics alone doesn't inherently bring change. Although Whites may soon no longer be the majority, our systems and power structure are rooted in that history, and as we've seen, challenging those systems is difficult and divisive. A portion of the US population is fearful of these demographic changes, worrying it will lessen their position or job prospects. There is a subset of Zs who harbor these fears as well, and the Proud Boys and Three Percenters actively work to recruit young people into their movements.

The oldest Zs were eleven when Barack Obama was elected president in 2008. They can't remember a time before we had a Black president. Zs acknowledge that this is significant, but because their goal is to elevate identity beyond race and gender, Obama being Black or Kamala Harris being Black and South Asian and female doesn't define them. Political pundits were shocked that Zs didn't universally mobilize behind Harris, but Zs looked beyond her race and gender to question her record on criminal justice. In the same way, many Zs look beyond Supreme Court Justice Amy Coney Barrett's gender to question her positions on sex discrimination in the workplace or safe and easily accessible healthcare for women.

Kamala Harris is a great example of the kind of racial amalgam that is completely familiar to Generation We. One in ten Gen Zs in the United States is multiracial and not necessarily with the kind of simple hyphenated combinations earlier generations were used to: perhaps they are a mixture of Black and South Asian, like Kamala, or of a Korean father and a Mexican mother.

Kids from blended families defy traditional definitions. They look at the race/ethnicity boxes on a required form: *Are you Hispanic? American Indian? Of Asian descent? White?* Sometimes the only box they can check is Other. Eventually, so many Americans will check Other that it will become the majority answer—in which case, calling it Other no longer makes sense. The boxes no longer apply because now Other simply means American.

BREAKING THE BINARY

Zs make clear distinctions between sex, gender, and sexual identity. Sex is the anatomy someone is born with. Gender is how you identify, as male, female, or outside of this binary. Sexual orientation is who you are physically attracted to: straight, gay, bisexual, and so on.

Zs are the first generation to broadly embrace that anatomy and gender are not only different but completely separate. Regardless of your biology, gender should be a chosen part of your identity, based on how you feel on the inside and choose to express yourself. Just because you were born without a penis doesn't mean you are destined to live life according to "feminine" conventions. As a twenty-year-old from Texas explains, "You're born with your sex, but your gender is something that's placed upon you almost without consent, whereas we should have the freedom to decide how we want to approach the world and how the world should get to know us."

Gen Z believes gender is largely a social construct that has been created by society over time, assigning arbitrary expectations on how one's biological sex translates into how one should look and behave. Zs are adamant that this social construct is no longer relevant today and actively reject it. One eighteen-year-old from Michigan explained, "Gender is a social construct that doesn't apply to everyone. Some people identify as the gender they were born as, and some don't. Gender has been used mainly to divide and stereotype us in the past, and that just doesn't appeal to me."

In our work, about one-third of Zs define themselves as nonbinary,[45] meaning they don't want to be identified as strictly male or female. Zs embrace gender as a spectrum, and although some nonbinary Zs may identify as trans (having an internal identity that doesn't correspond to their birth sex), others may operate more fluidly (embracing a range of gender across the spectrum) while others simply reject gender norms as a point of principle. They object to the rules of the game—even if they don't want to play the game anyway.

Zs are broadening the options and language around gender. They are ushering in a tolerant and inclusive mindset that feels revolutionary.

A clear majority of Zs—59 percent—believe that forms like the census should include options other than male and female.[46] Forward-thinking companies have adapted already, embracing a wider variety of gender and sexuality indicators. The dating app Tinder offers fifty gender-identity options. No other generation is as comfortable as Generation We with complex and diverse definitions of gender and sexuality. Even if they live in real-world communities with few or no apparent deviations from the traditional Norman Rockwell version of American life, their digital feeds normalize diversity in a way other generations never have.

---

45   Research by ZSpeak by Global Mosaic, July 2020.

46   Kim Parker, Nikki Graf, and Ruth Igielnik, "Generation Z Looks a Lot Like Millennials on Key Social and Political Issues," Pew Research Center's Social & Demographic Trends Project, Pew Research Center, January 17, 2019.

Zs believe everyone should be able to explore and choose how they want to show up in the world. Just because someone was born with male or female anatomy shouldn't impact how they behave or dress, the jobs they do, or who they love. For Zs, exploring their gender is just a part of growing up, of trying different things and seeing how you feel on the inside. Today, they see a variety of gender identities on TV, in movies, on social media and can relate to the people they see on screen. If you can see it, you can be it.

The fact that one-third of Zs want to live somewhere in the non-binary reflects this exploration. They see gender identity as an active process. They grow up exploring wearing different kinds of clothing and behaving in different ways. Globally, a quarter of Gen Z say they may change their gender identity at least once during their lifetime.[47] This doesn't necessary mean that they will, but they embrace the right to do so. As a fourteen-year-old from Georgia said, "I feel as though I am a male because I was born as one. However, I am still young, so that could change."

It's worth noting that the vast majority of Zs—about 70 per-cent—still identify as what they call cisgender. In other words, the gender they identify with matches their birth anatomy. But that doesn't mean they don't broadly support their peers who identify otherwise. One twenty-year-old from South Carolina explained, "Things have changed. Gender isn't a coin with only two sides. It's a spectrum. And no matter what someone decides to call themselves, whether it's male, female, or something in between, they are valid and it is important to respect them for what they are."

---

47   Thom Waite, "Read Gucci and Irregular Labs' Latest Report on Gender Fluidity in Gen Z," Dazed, December 22, 2018, https://www.dazeddigital.com/life-culture/article/42698/1/read-gucci-irregular-labs-latest-report-on-gender-fluidity-gen-z.

THE IDENTITY WHEEL

Zs are leading nothing short of an identity revolution.

In the United States, it's now common for Zs to start their school year by filling in an Identity Wheel. According to the University of Michigan, "The Identity Wheel worksheet encourages students to identify social identities and reflect on the various ways those identities become visible or more keenly felt at different times, and how those identities impact the ways others perceive or treat them." The wheel has different sections for race, ethnicity, socioeconomics, gender, sex, sexual orientation, national origin, first language, religion, age, and ability. The space in the middle of the wheel invites students to examine which identities they think about most or least, and which have the strongest impact on how they view themselves and how others view them. The wheel can be used to facilitate discussion among peers or simply as a tool for reflection.

As with gender, the Identity Wheel invites Zs to think about their identity not as something bestowed upon them at birth but something they have the opportunity to create and shape. It's the basis for an open discussion about the diversity of identities, which in turn builds community and encourages empathy.

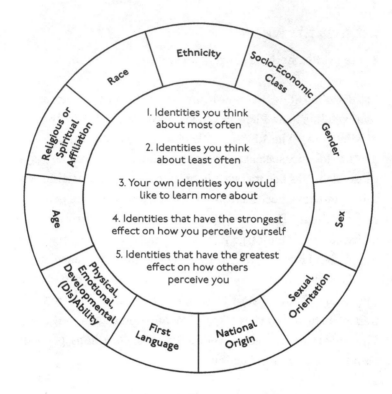

Ethnicity

Socio-Economic Class

Race

Gender

Religious or Spiritual Affiliation

Sex

Age

Sexual Orientation

Physical, Emotional, Developmental (Dis)Ability

First Language

National Origin

1. Identities you think about most often

2. Identities you think about least often

3. Your own identities you would like to learn more about

4. Identities that have the strongest effect on how you perceive yourself

5. Identities that have the greatest effect on how others perceive you

EVOLVING MASCULINITY

As we've discussed, for Generation We gender isn't confined to convention, and gender expression is fluid rather than static. Any individual, regardless of their sex, gender identity, or sexual preference, can embrace both their feminine and masculine sides, on one day wearing a skirt and the next, a suit.

But Zs across the spectrum are specifically challenging the traditional expression of masculinity.

Just as they see gender as a social construct, Zs see traditional expressions of masculinity as part of a patriarchal construct that has been created over time to maintain the power structure. They see the patriarchy as a system erected on arbitrary expectations of how biological sex translates into the way a person looks, behaves, and can treat others. It has historically created fewer rights and opportunities for females as compared to males, and by doing so, it limits everyone.

As one sixteen-year-old from Florida observed, "These systems only exist to hurt or benefit some people more than others. Never feel the need to prove yourself for a construct that will constantly shift its definitions and inevitably fade away into obscurity."

Zs have grown up with the #MeToo movement. They've heard the stories about toxic masculinity, misogyny, and the sordid details around Bill Cosby, Jeffrey Epstein, and Harvey Weinstein. They heard the tape of Donald Trump talking about grabbing women. They saw the sexual misconduct allegations against Brett Kavanaugh—and then his confirmation as a Justice on the US Supreme Court.

When previous generations were young, there was little discussion about what it meant to be a man. Any debate was likely couched in terms of movie or sports heroes. Generation We no longer has such unnuanced ideals of masculinity. As a generation, they are redefining what masculinity looks like, openly discussing and calling out examples that feel toxic to them, from a celebrity's music video to a social media post from a peer. As a nineteen-year-old from Wisconsin told us, "I'm a cisgender man. My pronouns are he, him, and his. But even though I identify as a cisgender man, I do not fit into society's expectations of masculinity."

Most men of all generations would reject traditional expressions of masculinity if they thought Harvey Weinstein (and the system that protected him) was the poster boy.

AN IMPERATIVE

There's an argument that we all start out without biases. That's why you see young kids playing and befriending each other without any concept of race or gender. In this view, humans are naturally inclusive but learn to become less inclusive as they get older, due to social conditioning and education that encourage them to classify others into groups and then accept or reject those groups depending on a whole range of factors.

Generation We believes that it's not just possible to return to this inherent inclusivity but absolutely imperative.

Older generations sometimes see that as nothing more than Pollyanna naïveté.

Zs are not only growing up themselves as the most racially diverse and gender-fluid generation. They are also already actively fighting for the inherent rights they believe everyone deserves, in both the racial and gender spaces.

Zs are building on a longer trajectory of progress in these areas, but think about what they've witnessed just in their short lifetimes. Many Zs can't remember a time before same-sex marriage became legal in 2015. In 2020, the Supreme Court ruled that the 1964 Civil Rights Act also protects LGBTQ+ employees from discrimination in the workplace.[48] That same year, Pete Buttigieg became the first openly gay candidate to run for president. Pride has grown from a minority event to a full monthlong celebration with big brands like Nike and Adidas promoting Pride clothing and Pride shoes.

---

48   Nina Totenberg, "Supreme Court Delivers Major Victory to LGBTQ
     Employees," NPR, June 15, 2020, https://www.npr.org/2020/06/15/863498848/
     supreme-court-delivers-major-victory-to-lgbtq-employees.

At the same time, Generation We has witnessed not only the continuation of gender prejudice and violence but, in many cases, its rise. The trans bathroom debates generated hateful outrage, and 2020 saw the highest number of reported murders of trans women to date.

The conversations around gender rights are loud and constant—and very complex.

Although these conversations expand on the gender work done by the women's movement or the LGBTQ+ protests of the seventies and eighties, they also include exponentially more perspectives, as those movements were more rooted in the binary, whereas now, there are infinite positions on a spectrum.

At least that is how older generations tend to see it: as a topic so complex it is unfathomable.

Zs don't see it as complicated. Put an end to the ridiculousness of it all. Just let people be who they are and give everyone equal rights. No elements of someone's self-identity should work against them when it comes to the opportunities they are afforded or the way they're treated.

The future implications of a generation that is as diverse and inclusive as Gen Z are inspiring. They will continue fighting for equity on multiple fronts. Their determination to fashion not only their own identities but also their collective identity is testament to their faith in their ability to shape all elements of their lives. And as we'll see in the next chapter, *this* leads to great creativity.

CHAPTER 5

The Most Creative Generation

"I want to work as a creator. My definition of a 'creator' is some-one who uses their creative skills and fundamental thinking to influence and help others in a positive way. Given a platform and a voice to speak up, you can truly change the world with how you think and why you think that way."

—SEVENTEEN-YEAR-OLD Z, MINNESOTA

What did you want to be when you grew up?

An astronaut? A firefighter? A veterinarian or a doctor? An inventor? Maybe a movie star or a professional athlete?

Whatever it was, it definitely wasn't the number one answer most eight- to twelve-year-olds gave in a recent survey. The youngest Zs want to be a vlogger or a YouTuber. More kids—29 percent—want to be an online creator than a professional athlete (23 percent) or musician (19 percent).[49] And as we'll see,

---

49 Paige Leskin, "American Kids Want to Be Famous on YouTube, and Kids in China Want to Go to Space: Survey," Business Insider, July 17, 2019, https://www.businessinsider.com/american-kids-youtube-star-astronauts-survey-2019-7.

this isn't just youthful naïveté: posting videos is the first step to building an empire in the growing creator economy.

Another poll, by Gallup, found that 24 percent of students in grades 1–12 had already started a business of some kind.[50] It might be crafting sticker designs on RedBubble or selling custom-made jewelry on Etsy, but somehow each of these kids traded and earned money.

Creativity is the touchstone of Generation We. It conditions their approach to everything: fashioning their own identity, using activism to make the world a better place, or creating their own businesses to disrupt a system to which they have little loyalty.

Some of that creativity comes from the energy of youth. From the imagination of sketching designs in the margins of their schoolwork or experimenting with makeup on TikTok or YouTube. From the enthusiasm of creating new virtual worlds on Minecraft or Animal Crossing. But like almost everything else that has to do with Generation We, it's linked directly to technology.

CONTENT GENERATORS

Gen Z grew up generating content online, and in doing so, they developed the creative skills they are now translating into systems and organizations that will shape our lives.

While millennials and older generations usually consume content, Zs prefer to create it. They're the touchscreen generation. They've had an interactive online experience since their parents

---

50 Jim Clifton and John Hope Bryant, "Forty Percent of 5th–12th Graders Plan to Start a Business," Gallup, April 5, 2021, https://news.gallup.com/opinion/chairman/208199/forty-percent-5th-12th-graders-plan-start-business.aspx.

first gave them an iPhone or a tablet to occupy them when they were very young.

In terms of social media, Gen X and older are the Facebook generations, mostly staying within their own digital echo chambers. Millennials are the Instagram generation, consuming beautiful images of camera-ready lives; Instagram fueled the rise of "influencers," though most millennials followed influencers rather than becoming one. Gen Z is the generation of TikTok and YouTube, platforms that democratized content creation via simple videos everyone could make—and the Zs did. Zs' social media experience has always been rooted in creation.

YouTube was launched in 2005 and came of age with Gen Z, who made it the most popular long-form video-sharing platform, with most videos between five and thirty minutes long (in contrast, TikTok is the most popular short-form platform, with videos only fifteen to sixty seconds long). Whereas older generations grew up watching highly produced cartoons or television shows, Zs grew up watching YouTube videos created in ordinary people's bedrooms and basements. Videos were historically low quality, recorded with a phone in one shot, and unedited.

Although there's still a lot of that, YouTube content has evolved as Zs have become more sophisticated. It's no longer just a collection of talking heads addressing the camera. Creators have their own channels, where they create their own programming, from nine-year-old Ryan Kaji, who showcases new toys on his channel, Ryan's World, and made $29 million in 2020 to a modern-day reality-sitcom format utilized by people like JoJo Siwa and Emma Chamberlin.[51]

---

51   Rupert Neate, "Ryan Kaji, 9, Earns $29.5m as This Year's Highest-Paid YouTuber," *The Guardian*, December 18, 2020, https://www.theguardian.com/technology/2020/dec/18/ryan-kaji-9-earns-30m-as-this-years-highest-paid-youtuber.

Zs never reach for an instruction manual, by the way. They never go to a product website. They never call a helpline. Whatever the problem may be, they find a video on YouTube to fix it.

TV requires production, professionals, and money; it's distant from viewers. Most YouTube stars started out with nothing but a camera phone. If you grew up watching YouTube videos, you grew up with the notion that videos are something made by ordinary people, not an elite set of creatives, and that you can do the same thing.

YouTube is largely how Zs are educated and entertained. Some 62 percent of Zs report being on YouTube every day, and 89 percent every week.[52]

TikTok is the number one app for Zs, but it has only been around since 2017, so many Zs posted their first content on YouTube. It might have been a DIY music video, a skit they created with their friends, a funny song, a clip of their dog, or a dance routine. It might have been their creations on Minecraft or a tour of a town they created on The Sims.

It's likely that barely anybody saw this video, but that doesn't make the endeavor any less creative.

This creation starts at a young age. Jules LeBlanc started posting her gymnastics routines on YouTube as a young child. She gathered followers, so she made clips of herself singing songs. Then she started writing and posting her own songs. By the time she was fifteen, Jules had 4 million subscribers on YouTube and is now an actor on Nickelodeon.

---

52   Jessica Baron, "The Key to Gen Z Is Video Content," *Forbes*, July 3, 2019, https://www.forbes.com/sites/jessicabaron/2019/07/03/the-key-to-gen-z-is-video-content/?sh=3638581d3484.

She parlayed posting videos into an acting career. And she is not alone. YouTube has created a pipeline from internet fame to TV or movie fame in the creator economy.

The idea of short-form videos began with Vine, which became popular when Zs were very young and is still part of older Zs' cultural lexicon. Vine videos were only six and a half seconds long. A similar app, musical.ly, featured mainly young teens singing songs or doing funny dances. (Vine eventually disappeared, and musical.ly was acquired by TikTok in 2017.)

Even from its infancy, short-form video launched many careers. When Vine was deactivated, many Vine creators turned to YouTube to produce longer-form videos while others took their comedy or writing skills to TV or movies. Jimmy Tatro, for example, went from Vine to creating the series *American Vandal* for Netflix and starring in blockbuster movies like *22 Jump Street* before headlining in the sitcom *Home Economics*. Vine comedian Demi Adejuyigbe became a writer on shows like *The Late Late Show with James Corden*, *The Amber Ruffin Show*, and *The Good Place*. These early creators were pioneers of bringing a specific brand of internet humor into the mainstream; now even *Saturday Night Live* sources talent from the online space. Gone are the days of scouts scouring late-night stand-up circuits: now they can stay home and watch the digital résumé of any up-and-coming comedian or writer on YouTube or TikTok.

Because phones are a constant for Zs, creativity is a constant. Even the school curriculum has changed. In my childhood, creativity was slotted into fourth-period art; today, teachers leverage Zs' digital creativity across subjects. Students may be asked to tell the story of *Romeo and Juliet* through a series of tweets or create dating profiles for the protagonists from *Pride and Prejudice*.

While posting videos on YouTube and TikTok is one of the most accessible forms of digital creativity for Zs, evolving technology has spawned unprecedented opportunities to be creators in gaming, graphic design, and music.

Look at the totally open-ended game Minecraft, which was the number one video game when Generation We was growing up. Minecraft is a blank canvas. Unlike previous video games, where players entered the makers' world, the Minecraft user creates their own world. That is the very essence of the game, which has no specific goals or rules. It's a game of building blocks where you never run out of blocks. You never have to wait until you get your allowance to finish building your tower. Players can choose to play alone, with friends, or even with strangers. They can spend months creating vast, intricate worlds.

The game suits Zs' unfettered creativity perfectly.

WE'RE ALL CREATORS NOW

TikTok encourages its users to think of themselves as creators. That's the language they use. In the world of TikTok, whenever someone posts something, they are a "creator."

TikTok makes the process so easy that 83 percent of users have posted a video.[53] In other words, 83 percent of TikTok users are "creators."

---

53 Brandon Doyle, "TikTok Statistics—Everything You Need to Know [Feb 2021 Update]," Wallaroo Media, February 6, 2021, https://wallaroomedia.com/blog/social-media/tiktok-statistics/.

And it doesn't require anything other than a camera; no lighting, no sound engineering. The quality isn't important. And you can create anything you want.

Generally, you can be as silly, or as honest, or as provocative as you feel. Just put it all up there. Nothing's excluded. Everyone's invited.

The average user spends fifty-two minutes a day on TikTok, and the average user under sixteen years old averages eighty minutes.[54]

That's a lot of short-form videos.

There are huge incentives. Charli D'Amelio was fifteen when she first posted videos of herself dancing in May 2019; by November 2020, she became the first TikTok creator to amass 100 million followers: that's more than the population of the Roman Empire at its height. Online success translated to opportunities outside of TikTok: D'Amelio danced at the Super Bowl, has written a book, and has a signature drink at Dunkin Donuts nationwide. She reportedly earned $4 million from sponsorships in 2020— and just a year earlier, no one knew who she was.

TikTok encourages Zs to explore many different sides of themselves—and they are far less likely than previous generations to glom onto one identity early on. They like to keep exploring. Like Jules LeBlanc, who evolved from being a gymnast to a singer-songwriter to an actor, TikTok lets people redefine themselves publicly. Maybe I'm a designer, maybe I'm a comedian, maybe I'm a great makeup artist.

---

54 Ibid.

TikTok encourages this.

Not everyone gets to be Charli D'Amelio or Jules LeBlanc, but everyone gets the same freedom to create what they want. Without judgment.

In contrast, Zs see Instagram and Snapchat as highly corporate, controlled by White dudes in Silicon Valley who determine the rules. Zs see TikTok as being free from those unconscious (or conscious) biases that exist in algorithms and coding on other platforms. The Trump administration might have singled TikTok out as a tool of the Chinese state, but as far as Generation We is concerned, it's simply a forum where they can say whatever they want with little interference from omnipotent corporate forces.

Much as their phones are less a piece of hardware than a portal, TikTok is less a piece of software than an invitation to create—just as Minecraft was an open world ready to be built. A twenty-one-year-old from Michigan explained, "TikTok's openness to be creative and form communities is much more free and accessible than any other app," while a seventeen-year-old from Washington state said, "The best part about TikTok is its authenticity."

Generation We loves expressing themselves. No one will die wondering what their opinions are about...almost anything.

DON'T CALL US INFLUENCERS!

Zs make a clear distinction between creators—who include everyone—and influencers, who definitely don't.

For the past decade, consumers and brands have been obsessed with "influencers," individuals who amass huge numbers of followers on social media whose decisions they can affect. Although some influencers are celebrities, many are regular people who grew their base through aspirational, engaging content and interacting with their followers. One of the earliest examples was the explosion of "mommy bloggers" when millennials began having children; it soon became clear that their followers would often do or buy what the blogger suggested, opening a highly targeted way for advertisers to reach potential customers. Influencers essentially become their own brand and can build an empire through paid product placement and sponsorships. Being an influencer has become highly lucrative. Brands are predicted to spend up to $15 billion on influencer marketing in 2022.[55]

Most millennial influencers were less interested in exploring their creativity and more in creating a business by building a brand they could monetize. The patinaed, highly curated images of their lives are reminiscent of the gloss of advertising. To paraphrase the well-known saying, the business of being an influencer is indeed a business.

To Zs, influencer culture is an extension of the corporate advertising machine. In contrast, they reject gloss; they want *real*. They got into creating content as children (millennials were often in their twenties) and their creativity often reflects the unfettered joy of young kids, encouraged by their online toybox. Zs are passionate about creation for creation's sake. It's an extension of who they are: how they put themselves, their passions, their unique voice out into the world. Although successful cre-

55   Insider Intelligence, "Influencer Marketing: Social Media Influencer Market Stats and Research for 2021," Business Insider, January 6, 2021, https://www.businessinsider.com/influencer-marketing-report.

ators are just as likely to aspire to financial freedom as millennial influencers, their focus is more on their content than brand partnerships. Zs follow creators to engage with their work, not to see what products they're endorsing.

Being a creator is a huge Z dream: do what you love and get paid for it. As we'll see in Part II, the creator economy makes this possible.

NEW ROLE MODELS

Zs are on YouTube and TikTok virtually every day, so they have a lot of exposure to whatever YouTubers or TikTokers they follow. That degree of familiarity is the reason 70 percent of teenagers told a Google study that they can relate to YouTubers more than traditional celebrities. In the same study, 40 percent of teenagers said that their favorite creator understands them better than their friends.[56]

This underscores just how interactive the platforms are. They feel more like a community of friends than fandom. Everyone interacts. Followers leave messages and requests in the comment section and the creator responds, giving both sides agency and influence in the relationship.

The Google survey also found that 70 percent of Zs feel creators are the people who most change and shape culture.[57] Zs feel they have a relationship with creators they simply don't have with traditional celebrities—although, in fact, creators can generate

---

56 Warner Geyser, "Why YouTube Stars Are More Influential than Traditional Celebrities," Influential Marketing Hub, October 24, 2018, https://influencermarketinghub.com/youtube-stars-influential-traditional-celebrities/.

57 Ibid.

considerable wealth very quickly and enjoy pretty rarified and entitled lives compared to "normal" teenagers. Social media personalities have perfected this brand of relatability. Although celebrities were once revered for their glamour and separation from the masses, young celebrities are following the trend of greater accessibility, too.

Zs might have multiple social media accounts to explore their different identities. They might have a main TikTok or Instagram page and multiple others: one for music, say, one for their art, one for their photographs. They use different channels to create different kinds of content as they explore what they might be good at—the kind of things that are worthy of being in the world. Zs understand that creativity is a process, and they explore the process publicly. Unlike previous generations of artists who weren't seen in a gallery or musicians who weren't picked up by a label until they'd honed their craft, Zs share their evolution with their followers in an interactive way.

It's part of the same extraordinarily explorative mindset we see in their attitude toward gender.

SNAPCHAT

No generation has been raised with such a range of creative online tools as Generation We. The apps they use are designed to invite creativity.

As with TikTok, anyone who creates and posts something on Snapchat is essentially a creator. After TikTok and YouTube, Snapchat—an app for communicating with friends via ephemeral pictures—is where Zs spend most of their time online. Like other platforms, Snapchat provides the tools for users to make something for themselves. The key to Snapchat is that it opens directly on to the camera, which is an invitation to take, manipulate, and send photos. For older generations, digital communication uses words; Zs have a whole range of visual ways to communicate, from emojis to Bitmojis (personalized avatars) to custom Snapchat photos.

Snapchat comes loaded with filters, lenses, and other creativity tools so users can write on their pictures, add stickers, or customize images. It's another step up in self-expression. It's the digital version of doodling for your friends. On steroids.

Augmented reality (AR) face lenses allow users to give themselves freckles or puppy ears or change the color of their hair. World lenses mean creators can place themselves in Paris, perhaps with rainbows surrounding the Eiffel Tower, swimming with sharks in the ocean, or even in Bart Simpson's bedroom.

Snapchat's face lenses and world lenses became so popular that users can now download Lens Studio to create AR lenses themselves, which they can publish to be used by potentially millions of other Snapchatters. Today, many Zs are creating their own AR lenses, and a few have been able to turn it into a living. For example, a British trans teen named Tyler Woodford, who is now an official Snapchat Lens Studio creator, specifically designs AR lenses for trans and LGBTQ+ users to be more inclusive of a broader range of identity. He also designs clothing and accessories, identifiable by his slogan, "UR a trans girl."

Another official Lens Studio creator, Benjamin Paruzynski, started creating AR lenses for musicians. He creates AR album covers for bedroom musicians, helping them look more professional when they release their music. His album cover for

Lebanese singer-songwriter Bazzi got hundreds of millions of views, enabling Paruzynski to found his own company, ChAR Digital, to provide content directly for labels like Atlantic Records.

Snapchat's own research underlines how the platform feeds the most creative generation. More than half of Gen Z (56 percent) use their social media to express themselves creatively, and nearly the same number (55 percent) said they could be more creative on social media than offline (although, even offline, 51 percent of Zs believe they are more creative than previous generations). Just under half (48 percent) regularly engage in creative activities, such as meme creation, and about a quarter of Zs (27 percent) have hacked apps to be able to do something that isn't normally feasible, like using an editing tool to add to an existing collage or using an audio app to add a layer to prerecorded music.[58]

Yes, they're expressing their creativity by hacking the creative apps that will allow them to be more creative.

(A quick aside: 55 percent of Gen Zs say they prefer content that allows them to choose the plot line as they go along. Already, Netflix has created two different shows that have a "choose your own adventure" format with countless endings that are up to the viewer. *Black Mirror: Bandersnatch* (2018) allowed the viewer to make choices for the characters, from what cereal they ate in the morning to major plot twists. *Unbreakable Kimmy Schmidt* (2020) followed that up with a highly interactive storyline. Just imagine what TV shows or movies will look like in the future.)

58   Jessica Rapp, "Into Z Future: Understanding Generation Z, the Next Generation of Super Creatives," JWT Intelligence Group, 2020, https://gertkoot.files.wordpress.com/2019/06/into-z-future_understanding-gen-z_the-next-generation-of-super-creatives-1.pdf.

INNOVATIVE ENTREPRENEURS

Generation We is constantly creating in highly innovative ways. They typically use their digital fluency to evolve from simple images or videos to multimedia multidisciplinary endeavors as they grow older. That helps them build influence and grow their followers until at least some are able to monetize their creativity.

Perhaps they create art, clothing, or accessories to sell on Depop, a mobile marketplace where many Zs sell their digital creations. Or maybe they make short films or vlogs about themselves.

They have access to a remarkable mash-up of creativity that simply wasn't available to previous, nondigital generations.

Instead of launching a journalistic career through a highly coveted *The New York Times* internship, Zs create e-zines, or digital magazines, from their bedrooms and dorm rooms. E-zines covering every potential niche have flooded the digital space. *Gen-Zine* was launched by nineteen-year-old Anushka Joshi when she was in college to address contemporary issues like gender, race, and politics, specifically through the lens of Gen Z. Before the 2020 election, she created an eighty-eight-page digital edition as a guide for first-time voters that was widely picked up in the traditional media.

This kind of self-publishing allows for the creative works to be owned by the creator and brings together creativity and activism, diversity and inclusivity: the intersectional touchstones of Generation We.

It also reflects their entrepreneurial nature. Three-quarters of Gen Z—76 percent—believe they can turn hobbies and what they love into a successful full-time business and that they can accomplish this all online.[59]

Unlike millennials, who grew up during a time of greater economic stability and prosperity—the shit hit the fan after most were in college—Zs have grown up with parents who lived through the Great Recession of 2008. Their parents are more likely to work in a gig economy with unsecured income and no benefits.

Their parents' experience, combined with unpredictable economic cycles, has made Zs cynical about traditional employment. In addition, when they look at the millennials before them, they see how their predecessors have been crippled by student debt.

It's natural for Zs to wonder why they would sign up for a traditional approach to education or employment, when they've seen so many of their peers hacking that system and experiencing success as creators.

It's not just the money that inspires Zs. It's the opportunity to put something out into the world, an extension of yourself and your passions. When Zs are asked why they want to be entrepreneurs, they talk about wanting to be creative, wanting to have freedom, wanting to lead a purposeful life, and wanting to have a positive impact.

It would be naive to think Zs aren't concerned about money. The creator economy is in its infancy, and Zs are pioneering models for monetization that will increasingly legitimize this as

---

59   Deep Patel, "How Gen Z Will Shape the Future of Business," *Forbes*, April 18, 2017, https://www.forbes.com/sites/deeppatel/2017/04/18/how-gen-z-will-shape-the-future-of-business/?sh=5036382876e8.

a career. It's also worth saying that Zs are pragmatic enough to see entrepreneurship as a potential survival mechanism in an education and job market that no longer serves them.

Creative destruction.

For all the obstacles they face, Zs have no fear. Boldness is one of their generational hallmarks.

When I look at my own story, I didn't start my first company, Global Mosaic, until I had more than ten years' experience and had completed a graduate degree. Until then, I wasn't sure that I was ready. A Z would think, *Why bother with all that? I've had the idea, so why don't I just see if I can do it?*

Some might crash and burn, but others will thrive. And it all starts with creativity. Where millennials may have said, "I want to earn a lot of money" or "I want to be a startup millionaire," Zs set out as kids having fun online, then they start creating, and then those skills evolve into creative outlets that earn them money.

Look at the story of Billie Eilish, whose rise to fame as a pop star is a uniquely Z story. She was making music in her bedroom with her brother when she put a song up on the music-hosting website SoundCloud to share with her teacher. The song went viral and became the most popular song on the site. She made her first album in her childhood bedroom with DIY sound equipment, produced by her brother.

Eilish was the first artist born in the twenty-first century to have a number one hit, partly because she was willing to explore new trajectories of what's possible in the music industry, and grew her fan base organically on social media.

Eilish is just one product of a new, more egalitarian era of music that gives more agency to the artist. Chicago-based Chance the Rapper famously became the first artist to win a Grammy in 2017 without ever selling a physical album. More and more artists are choosing to make their music independently to retain full control over their artistry and image. As soon as artists were able to burn their own CDs to sell to their friends, music labels' power began to decline. Now a musician can easily upload their own work to a site like SoundCloud or Spotify to instantly reach a massive audience. Eilish's first upload to SoundCloud, "Ocean Eyes," has been listened to 47.6 million times on that app alone.

Today, she's one of the biggest music stars in the world, not only because of her talent, but because she has the agency to truly carve out her own space, free of industry manipulation. The creator economy has flipped the power structure that once silenced and commodified its artists.

A powerful example of this transformation at work was Taylor Swift re-releasing her *Fearless* album in April 2021 to gain legal ownership of her own music. The album was originally released in 2008 by Big Machine Records, who then sold the master recordings to Ithaca Holdings, who later resold them to Shamrock Holdings. Swift did not own her own discography, all royalties being collected by Shamrock Holdings. Swift is setting a precedent by re-recording her albums and reclaiming her agency, free of record label control.

We're at a critical pivot in independent creativity. This new system eliminates the need for gatekeepers to an industry, and democratizes who gets to deem a song or a piece of visual art or a publication worthy. The gates are open. Now we all get to decide for ourselves.

Part II

The Coming Transformation

CHAPTER 6

Beyond Gender

"We don't really have any preconceptions about what gender is and what it should be, and as a generation, we just want to treat people well, and if that means accepting who they really are, then that's what that means. So we don't feel like there's a right and a wrong the way older generations might have been raised, we just haven't, so we're accepting."

—SEVENTEEN-YEAR-OLD Z, TENNESSEE

A lot of things trigger conservative firebrand Candace Owens, so perhaps it was little surprise in November 2020 when she tweeted her dismay at the "feminization" of Western men, predicted the downfall of society, and issued a rallying cry: "Bring back manly men."

The outrage may have been par for the course, but the trigger was not. *Vogue* magazine had put an image of a man wearing a dress on its cover. Not just any man, but the British pop star Harry Styles, who has 38 million followers on Instagram. And not just any dress: in fact, a lacy Gucci ballgown.

Even if you ignore the thousands of Z males who began posting images of themselves in dresses or skirts to support Styles (who, at twenty-six, is a few years older than Generation We), it's clear that Owens is fighting a battle that's already been lost. Generation We has already changed the way everyone engages with gender, by rejecting the binaries of male and female in favor of individual identity. And in so doing, sending a tremor of nervousness through older people who were brought up to believe that male and female are mutually exclusive opposites (or that one is from Mars, the other from Venus).

The majority of Zs say their gender doesn't define them, and it certainly doesn't dictate what they wear. As a term of classification, gender seems as irrelevant to them as classifying athletes by the color of their eyes. Gender is far less important than expressing yourself authentically. For Zs, clothes are a way to do that.

In the interview accompanying his *Vogue* cover, Styles said, "What's really exciting is that all of these lines are just kind of crumbling away. And when you take away there's clothes for men and there's clothes for women, once you remove those barriers, you open up the arena in which you can play...It's like anything. Any time you're putting barriers up in your own life, you're just limiting yourself. There's so much joy to be had in play with clothes...It just becomes this extended part of creating something."

The contrast between views could hardly be starker: a harbinger of the end of Western civilization on the one hand; creativity, joy, and play on the other.

Generation We stands solidly with Harry Styles.

Gender is one of the areas where people feel most confused by the changes being introduced by Generation We, which is why the backlash is so loud. (Just ask Candace Owens.)

But gender is also one of the areas where the influence of Zs will be most profound. Changing how people look and dress is just the start. Zs' ideas about gender will shape life for everyone: young families figuring out how to paint their nursery; grandparents looking for a birthday gift for their grandchild; a parent helping their son or daughter buy clothes for prom; students selecting a sorority or fraternity at university. Zs will influence how we interact with the opposite sex, how we perceive the roles of men and women, and how we create families and raise children. The same ideas will spill into clothing stores, movies and TV, politics, sports, the workplace, and advertising. Not to mention fashion magazines...

EMBRACING MULTIPLICITY

For Generation We, gender is neither inevitable nor prescriptive. In Part I of this book, I talked about gender as a social construct created by society. Zs also talk about gender as a "performance," meaning that it is a set of behaviors based on accepted norms of femininity and masculinity that are learned and then performed every day—from how you walk and the language you use to whether you are allowed to cry or express emotions.

Not only do Zs reject the construct; their fierce self-expression means they want to take charge of their own performance. Everybody gets to write their own script and stage cues.

Rather than binaries, Generation We thinks in terms of multiplicity, partly because they see the multitudes of gender expression on their feeds every day. In music, they see Billie

Eilish, whose pronouns are they/them, intentionally wearing baggie sweatshirts and sweatpants to reject the sexualization of earlier pop stars. They see Frank Ocean, a cisgender gay male, embrace his sensitivity and vulnerability through the love songs he's written about men he's dated. Gone are the conventions of previous "female" or "male" musicians.

Little wonder that Zs believe in playing across the entire arc of self-expression. No one has to look or act like a woman or a man just because they happened to be assigned that designation at birth.

As Harry Styles says, gender expression is about removing barriers and embracing gender as play.

GENDER VERSUS SEXUAL ORIENTATION

Harry Styles is a cisgender man (he identifies with his birth sex as a male). He is not trans (with a gender identity different from his birth sex). He is not gay (sexually attracted to other men). For Zs, exploring gender expression is open to everybody. Just because a Z is on the binary doesn't mean they're any more likely to accept gender-based conventions about how they have to look or act.

Wearing a dress doesn't mean that a man is gay. Or trans. Or anything else.

However, it's important to note that society doesn't celebrate everyone's expression and creativity equally. The trans community, in particular, is met with criticism and even violence for dressing as they wish. The rapper Kid Cudi (a straight cisgender male) performed a tribute to Kurt Cobain (the deceased frontman of the '90s rock band Nirvana) on *Saturday Night Live* in April 2021 wearing a floral dress reminiscent of a dress the anti-establishment Cobain had worn in the early '90s to challenge gender boundaries. The tribute was largely celebrated online, but the LGBTQ+ community pointed out a double standard: cisgender straight men now receive praise for wearing a dress, while trans people have been bullied or even killed for wearing the same thing. As trans model and activist Munroe Bergdorf wrote on Instagram following the event, "As fab as it is to see cisgender straight men embracing femininity through fashion and all that it symbolizes...they also won't face nearly as much hatred or the physical danger that visibly queer folk will when they do the exact same thing."

One online response read, "For cis hetero men it's a trend, a costume...For trans people it's life or death." At the time of the post, fifteen transgender people had already been murdered in 2021.[60]

Here, it's important to return to the distinctions between biological sex, gender, and sexual orientation. We've been talking mainly about gender, but sexual orientation is another layer.

Although the science on these concepts is ever growing, sexual orientation has been accepted as a scientific given: it is taken that a person's biological wiring determines to whom they are sexually attracted. Critically, this is the legal basis for US court decisions that have extended LGBTQ+ rights. Sexual orientation is distinct from one's sexual organs or gender identity, adding to the exponential possibilities.

---

60 "Fatal Violence against the Transgender and Gender Non-conforming Community in 2021," Human Rights Campaign, 2021, https://www.hrc.org/resources/fatal-violence-against-the-transgender-and-gender-non-conforming-community-in-2021.

A cisgender man—whose male gender corresponds to his sexual biology—could have a homosexual orientation. A transgender female, who was assigned male at birth but identifies as a woman, might have a heterosexual orientation, meaning that she's attracted to the opposite sex—which in this case would mean males.

Little wonder some people feel confused, as the language and range of options seem to be proliferating with each passing day. Although I can reflect this particular point in time, no doubt the language and concepts in this space will have evolved further by the time you hold this book in your hands.

Zs are more likely to accept different sexual orientations without judgment, and some evidence suggests this tolerance has led to more sexual exploration, but it's difficult to tell how significant it might be. Many biographies of the past 150 years suggest that young people have often experimented with their own sex but that that exploration doesn't always extend into older age.

It's true that a greater number of Zs are identifying as bisexual or pansexual, but again it's difficult to know whether this reflects a rise in the actual incidence of the behavior, which after all, has always existed or simply a rise in the ability to express it publicly.

Bisexuality became a well-known concept in the second half of the twentieth century, acknowledging that people could be sexually attracted to both men and women. The more recent rise of the term "pansexual" reflects the inclusion of nonbinary identities. Although bisexuality is still within the gender binary (men/women), pansexuality means one can be attracted to anyone anywhere along the full gender spectrum.

Pansexuality hit the mainstream when the TV comedy *Schitt's Creek* first featured a pansexual character, David. (This was back in 2015; since then, bisexual and pansexual characters have cropped up increasingly on TV and in the movies.) After a hookup with a female friend (who previously thought he was gay), she remarks, "I only drink red wine, and up until last night I was under the impression that you too only drank red wine, but I guess I was wrong?" David replies, "I do drink red wine, but I also drink white wine. And I've been known to sample the occasional rosé. And a couple of summers back I tried a merlot that used to be a chardonnay, which got a bit complicated. I like the wine and not the label."

FASHION AS ART

The key is replacing self-oppression with self-expression. For Zs, self-expression is another form of creativity—and we've already seen that they're the most creative generation. So fashion simply becomes a wearable expressive art that doesn't suggest anything about the wearer's sex, gender, or sexual orientation.

Western culture has historically had strict rules around gender and how men and women are to dress (this is less so in Indian, Native American, and some Indigenous cultures, where gender and gender expression were historically more fluid). US history has at different times included legislation barring women from wearing trousers and criminalizing men for wearing dresses or makeup. These "cross-dressing" laws made it unlawful for any person to be found in clothing not customarily worn by his or her sex, specifically addressing fears of gay, lesbian, or trans folk.

Such laws have been dropped or struck down over time, but the cultural norms they reflect changed more slowly. As recently as the 1960s, men were chastised for having long hair and dress codes at workplaces and schools were just beginning to allow women to wear pants.

Zs are blowing up any cultural norms that still exist around clothing.

To older generations, that might imply fashion will become androgynous, with everyone gravitating toward the center and wearing purely functional clothing (similar to some of the unisex experiments of designers in the 1960s). Nothing could be further from the truth.

Generation We is about increasing options, not reducing them. There will be an explosion of creativity at both ends of the fashion spectrum. Clothing will be as feminine or masculine as ever—Harry Styles's Gucci ballgown would be hyperfeminine even for a cis female but will no longer be worn only by women or men. It's open to anyone. A clothing store becomes a big playground with no restrictions or boundaries.

Older Zs are creating their own clothing lines, and Z consumers have also pushed established brands toward a more fluid approach. Even Nordstrom, whose mass-market popularity depends on it leaning a little conservative, launched a nonbinary clothing line in 2020.[61]

Most of the stores Zs like, such as Urban Outfitters, still have a men's section and a women's section. It's no real wonder, as they tend to be run by older generations, but Zs just ignore the sections and shop the whole store.

---

61   Erika Harwood, "Eileen Fisher Teamed Up with Nordstrom on a Gender-Neutral, Sustainable Collection," Nylon, January 10, 2020, https://www.nylon.com/eileen-fisher-nordstrom-pop-in.

As we'll see in Chapter 9, Zs love thrift stores. That's partly an ecological preference for reusing clothes rather than buying new, but it's also because thrift stores democratize gender. As a rule, thrift stores take a minimal approach to virtually every task, and the first distinction to be thrown out the window is male versus female. Many thrift stores sort clothes into pants, skirts and dresses, jeans, sweatshirts, shoes and then let customers get on with it.

Zs love the freedom. It makes a shopping trip more of an expedition into the unknown. And it will undoubtedly influence other stores to change the way they are organized.

One collateral victim, by the way, will be the so-called pink tag, where the jeans and sweatshirts in the women's department are the same as those in the men's department but more expensive. (Because, well...just because: women's clothes have always been more expensive than men's.) It may be that dedicated women's or men's stores will disappear (bye-bye, Brooks Brothers) and be replaced by retailers that offer a range of masculine and feminine styles for everyone. Or stores might define themselves more by style than by the gender of the wearer: streetwear, athletic wear, workwear, formal wear, and so on.

But first, they have to get the kids out of the thrift store.

WHAT A DRAG

Partly as a consequence of their love of fashion and gender play as an artform, Zs have destigmatized drag and taken it into the mainstream. Drag culture has traditionally been relegated to the underground, but *RuPaul's Drag Race* (which is the most awarded reality show on TV, with nineteen Emmy wins) has brought drag into millions of living rooms. The tropes of self-expression, sassiness, and confidence, together with RuPaul's closing message each episode—"If you can't love yourself, how the hell are you gonna love somebody else?"—have become a source of inspiration for Zs both in and outside the binary.

Drag hasn't only infiltrated our TVs. *Drag Race* alumni (and many other queens outside of the show) have gone on to create their own makeup lines (Trixe Cosmetics by Drag All Stars winner Trixe Mattel, Kim Chi Beauty by Season 7 Top 3 finalist Kim Chi); performed on Broadway (Peppermint in Head over Heels); walked major runways (Gigi Gorgeous and Jada Essence Hall for Savage X Fenty); and stood up and spoke out not only for LGBTQ+ issues but issues around racial justice, criminal justice reform, and sexual assault advocacy for men (an often overlooked chapter of the #MeToo movement).

For Generation We, drag isn't only an art form and an escape. Investigating drag and its history has introduced many Zs to the struggles of the LGBTQ+ pioneers who helped win freedom of self-expression across the gender spectrum. What they have learned has given them a newfound respect for those who faced down ridicule, felt the harsh eyes of hatred on them as they walked down the street, took beatings from thugs and police alike, or dared to express themselves in the face of oppression.

MAKEUP FOR MEN

Makeup is on a similar trajectory to fashion, with divisions disappearing between masculine and feminine. Male Zs have channels on YouTube and TikTok where they are blowing up the idea that makeup is only for females. James Charles was fifteen years old in December 2015, when he pioneered makeup tutorials on YouTube; a year later, he became the first "male CoverGirl" for *CoverGirl* magazine. Charles, whose pronouns are he/him, has parlayed wearing makeup into a career. Within five years, he was the most subscribed male beauty guru in the world and his YouTube channel had 25.5 million subscribers and counting.

Charles didn't invent men wearing makeup, but he expanded the platform, taking makeup tutorials out of the bathroom and creating an online empire that inspired a generation of younger Zs to experiment and launch their own makeup tutorials and product lines. Meanwhile, nail polish has become part of a normalized look for many males, popularized from a reemerging punk aesthetic originally inspired by artists like David Bowie, Kurt Cobain, Keith Richards, and Steven Tyler. Celebs from Marc Jacobs to rappers Bad Bunny, Lil Yachty, and A$AP Rocky have embraced "nail art" as another nongendered form of self-expression. As Bad Bunny said, "I'm not telling people to paint your nails or color your hair or do this or that. I'm simply saying, do what makes you happy and to never limit yourself."

It's not androgyny. It's finding new forms of creativity by coloring outside the lines.

RELATIONSHIPS AND FAMILIES

As Generation We moves beyond gender, there will be a far greater impact than how people dress. A social shift this profound will inevitably impact relationships and families, as well as shaping the nebulous ideas of femininity and masculinity Zs will hand down to their kids, which will then become the bedrock values for the succeeding generation and the ideas they hand on in turn.

Regardless of who the partners are in a relationship—straight people, gay people, nonbinary people, pansexual people—they will have much more freedom to define their roles than in the past. A powerful article in *The Atlantic* several years ago[62] found that same-sex marriages were happier than heterosexual marriages, partly because heterosexual relationships came with set gender expectations on who would do what. Same-sex marriages don't have the same conventions, so couples are empowered to have more open conversations about expectations and roles: *What are you good at? What do you want to do? Who's better at the finances? Who's better at the child-rearing? Who prefers doing laundry?*

It's no coincidence that most Zs (and most millennials) describe their significant other as their partner. Not as their wife, husband, girl- or boyfriend, but as their partner.

This language reflects the idea that individuals come together as equals to build a life together and get to decide the role each plays based on their skills and preferences, not their gender. Even in straight relationships, there is much less emphasis on what Candace Owens would presumably call a manly man. *People* magazine's "Sexiest Man Alive" used to feature traditionally strapping men like Sean Connery, Tom Cruise, George Clooney, Harrison Ford, and Brad Pitt. Gen Z men who are considered sexy today—Timothée Chalamet, Pete Davidson, Harry Styles, or TikTok heartthrobs like Lil Huddy or any of the K-pop stars—don't look traditionally masculine at all. They tend to have a vulnerable, delicate look, sometimes described as the eboy aesthetic.

---

62 Liza Mundy, "The Gay Guide to Wedded Bliss," *The Atlantic*, June 18, 2013, https://www. theatlantic.com/magazine/archive/2013/06/the-gay-guide-to-wedded-bliss/309317/.

ZS AS PARENTS

I want to acknowledge that the oldest Zs have only just started to have children, so it's not entirely clear how they will approach marriage and child-rearing. There is such a limited dataset about their move into this next life stage that we can't really know what they'll be like as parents.

The first evidence is coming through, though. Although millennials invented baby gender-reveal parties, where family and friends were invited to a gathering to unveil and celebrate the gender of a fetus, it's no surprise Zs eschew this idea. In contrast, older Zs have taken to social media to explain that they will not announce the gender of their baby or, in some instances, will not treat the child as either male or female until the age of eighteen, giving the child time to figure out who they are and choose their own gender.

Aspiring to raise children in a gender-neutral way isn't particularly new, but Zs have a more nuanced approach best described as gender open or gender affirming. They don't want to guide children away from playing with dolls or trucks or even from liking pink or blue. They positively want their children to be able to explore all of it. That makes a lot more sense to Zs than gender neutrality, which implies taking away options and creating bland neutrality, which are both anathema to Generation We.

There's a lot of support around the idea of giving children the option to define themselves. (Zs love coining words, so they joke about calling a baby a "theirby.")

Another new model might be the one offered by the family of ex-Miami Heat NBA player Dwayne Wade and actress Gabrielle Union. As a young athlete steeped in locker room culture, Wade might be expected to be a traditional masculine role model. Instead, when Wade and his wife, Gabrielle, felt their child Zaya (who was assigned male at birth) might be transgender from a young age, they let her freely explore who she was. At age twelve, she came out as trans. As Dwayne explained, "She sat us down and said, 'Hey, I don't think I'm gay.' And she went down the list and said, 'This is how I identify myself. This is my gender identity. I identify myself as a young lady.'" Her parents responded by publicly supporting her decision in the press and have been speaking out on trans issues and inclusive parenting ever since.

However things continue to evolve, one thing is certain: this is the sort of story we'll hear more frequently as more Zs begin to have families.

FEMININE AND MASCULINE

Zs are a mash-up generation. Anyone can dress feminine and exude power. Anyone can dress masculine and cry in movies.

For a long time, male rappers have boldly embraced their sexuality. Zs love female rappers who have started to do the same, like Cardi B and Megan Thee Stallion, whose song "WAP" is an eye-popping anthem to female sexual empowerment. The song debuted at number one on *Billboard's* Hot 100 and was streamed 93 million times in its first week, a US record. Cardi and Megan's Grammy performance of the song was celebrated for its sex positivity while *Fox News* simultaneously hosted Candace Owens, who called the performance "a destruction of American values."

Zs loved the mash-up of femininity and empowerment.

Feminine expression isn't dead, but it's been freed from the shackles that tethered it to weakness and subservience, and to people born with girl parts. Femininity is something to be embraced by everyone, without limiting anyone's personal power. Zs reject the idea that anyone, anywhere on the spectrum has to act in a masculine way or dress in pantsuits or wear short haircuts to be perceived as smart or taken seriously. That's one reason they relate to AOC over Hillary Clinton. Hillary's generation thought they had to de-sex the way they looked.

Zs' attitudes toward masculinity are equally progressive.

As we saw in Chapter 4, Generation We have grown up surrounded by stories about toxic masculinity and reject any kind of gender-based violence or oppression. Zs found a spokesperson in Aly Raisman, the US gymnast who came forward at twenty-three years old as a survivor of routine abuse from the US gymnastics team's doctor, Larry Nassar. Her blistering speech at his 2018 trial went viral, as she bravely called him out: "I am here to face you, Larry, so you can see I have regained my strength, that I am no longer a victim. I am a survivor." She won the Arthur Ashe courage award for her testimony and has been a model for others to speak out against their oppressors.

It's accountability culture. Generation We simply don't make women part of their shtick. Masculinity isn't bad, but it's evolving. Zs are helping to create a more inclusive, nuanced expression of it that, like their expression of femininity, is open to anyone.

Zs don't believe in the end of femininity or masculinity; instead, they believe we need to move beyond previous limitations so we can each embrace both. As a twenty-one-year-old from

Texas explained, "We are all made up of a mixture of feminine and masculine. Acknowledging that and seeing depth to every person versus just 'man' versus 'women' is super important in everyone's personal development."

Z Voices

DESMOND NAPOLES: THE AMAZING

Thirteen-year-old Desmond Napoles (they/them) are known as "America's drag teen superstar" and are a runway model, published author, performer, actor, and recognized LGBTQ advocate.

Q: Hi, Desmond, can you tell us what got you into drag at such a young age?

A: Well, *RuPaul's Drag Race* got me into drag when I was two... and I think just being able to help people has been my passion ever since.

Q: What inspired you to write your recent children's book, *Be Amazing*?

A: I just knew that there were no books with LGBTQ history for kids. You know, there's always a boy in a dress, but how was the boy able to wear a dress, you know what I mean? I just wanted kids to know that back in those days, you couldn't be yourself... History has a way of repeating itself if we are not educated.

Q: What's the main message you wanted kids to get out of your book?

A: To be yourself, love everyone regardless of their opinions as long as they are not hurting anyone.

Q: Your motto is "Be yourself always." Can you talk more about that in your own words?

A: Being yourself always to me means loving yourself, first of all, being yourself, second of all, and paying the haters no mind because at the end of the day, as long as you're not hurting anyone or being disrespectful to anyone, just go for it.

Q: One of your other catchphrases is "Won't be erased." Could you explain a little bit of the background behind that?

A: It's about trans people and how trans people have always been erased or forgotten. And that's just not going to happen anymore. We're not forgotten. We're going to be accepted. And we're going to do what it takes to be accepted.

Q: What would you say to older generations who are just being introduced to the idea of gender being nonbinary?

A: Some people think there are only two genders. Some people think there are more than two genders. That's fine if you believe that, but just respect my pronouns, respect me, and treat me like a human being.

Q: Being gender fluid can be a new concept for a lot of older people. How would you describe gender fluidity?

A: Well, you don't identify as a boy or a girl. You switch. Sometimes you're a boy, sometimes you're a girl, sometimes you are neither.

Q: What do you think about the role of femininity and masculinity in 2021?

A: To me, a piece of fabric shouldn't be defined as masculine or feminine.

Q: What would you want to say to older generations about moving beyond gender?

A: Respect others' opinions. Don't be a boomer. Stop judging others and let me be myself.

CHAPTER 7

Diversity Is Our Superpower

"Celebrating diversity brings people together and helps build closer relationships. Embracing different people will help us learn about each other and understand one another. It can teach us their different cultures and values that we can learn to respect. Diversity will widen our perspective on issues we are facing today."

—SEVENTEEN-YEAR-OLD Z, CONNECTICUT

We've seen that Zs are the most ethnically and racially diverse generation in US history and are on their way to becoming the first non-White majority. But the numbers aren't the real story.

Diversity is more than numbers. The sum is bigger than its parts. A diversity of people, experiences, and perspectives can be harnessed to create a whole that is exponentially wiser, stronger, and more empathetic. Not to mention a hell of a lot more interesting.

Our history has treated diversity as something to be feared, at worst, and accommodated, at best. In contrast, Zs broadly embrace and celebrate their differences as one of their generation's defining characteristics.

They see diversity as a superpower.

And diversity is a far broader issue than race or ethnicity alone, even though racial equity remains one of Zs' touchstone issues. Zs have grown up sharing their personal stories online, building a platform of shared empathy for all kinds of diversity. Generation We push back against a culture that idealizes only limited types of beauty, body shape, and physical and mental ability. They reject single-point perspectives and see through one-dimensional stereotypes, because social media gives them daily access to the authentic, multidimensional lived experiences of their peers.

OMNICULTURALISM

The idea of the United States as a "melting pot" is well over 200 years old, acknowledging the steady immigration of people from diverse parts of the world. The term is a metaphor that implies assimilation, the melting away of differences in order to create a more homogenous society. Many of us remember older relatives who worked hard to learn English, to dress and act "American," hiding their cultural traditions so as not to betray their "first generation" status.

That view changed in recent decades with the evolution of multiculturalism, which acknowledged the United States as a place where multiple cultures can coexist yet remain distinct. This yielded a new set of metaphors for the nation, from a patchwork quilt to a mixed salad, but although it recognized differences, this approach still labeled populations as separate from one another. It left them all in their own boxes.

Zs reject such divisiveness. They simultaneously celebrate their differences, while creating a form of omniculturalism (*omni* meaning all).

Omniculturalism acknowledges that every human is inherently unique, not just in terms of race and gender but as an amalgam of all of our intersectional identities (think Identity Wheel). Our differences are precisely what unite us. In that way, omniculturalism is a celebration of all the ways to explore and experience the human condition. And to learn from each other in doing so.

It appeals to Zs who each want to be an individual and reject norms; they refuse to check one-dimensional boxes. Omniculturalism is rooted in empathy and sharing versus living in a subdivided world. It's an IRL echo of precisely the type of shared world Zs have created online.

Exposure to each other's diverse stories feeds an open-minded curiosity to learn more, and creates a sense of unity that erodes division across racial, gender, or other lines. It also reinforces the idea that everyone has their own unique, American experience. It turns out there are millions of individual boxes to check.

Zs love that idea.

Perhaps we're getting closer to what our founders intended: *E pluribus unum*, out of many, one.

CONNECTING BY STORIES

Stories are a particularly powerful connector for teens. They understand how it is to feel alienated, or scared, or unsure of their developing identity. And no generation has had the digital platform to broadly share their stories like Generation We. And boy, do they share.

On any given day, a Z's TikTok FYP (For You Page) is filled with video stories from young people all over the world: it might be a differently abled teen talking about dating, or a plus-sized teen giving clothing reviews, or a young Inuk sharing her Indigenous traditions.

Shina Novalinga is a twenty-two-year-old Inuk from northern Canada who, in March 2020, began sharing videos of her and her mother performing traditional throat singing, as well as talking about their culture and lifestyle. She now has more than 2 million followers on TikTok, and Zs probably know more than any previous generation about Inuk culture. As Shina explained, "A lot of people are getting used to it...and they see what we feel. It's just so beautiful to have this kind of connection with everyone."

Talk about representation. Every race and ethnicity, gender identity, body type, ability, and cultural tradition seems to be represented in these TikTok stories. And this kind of first-person storytelling is rooted in authenticity, providing a multidimensional, intersectional view of a person versus a one-dimensional stereotype. Yes, differently abled teens still get drunk and get ghosted by boys. Yes, plus-sized teens still love going out with their friends and trying bold fashion choices. Yes, straight guys love to experiment with makeup.

Zs put great stock in authentic storytelling and are correspondingly wary of the inauthentic. Previous generations may have learned about autism from watching *Rain Man*; about race from the *Cosby Show*; about Yuppies from *Friends*. Media execs decided what stories to tell about autism or race or youthfulness, even though they themselves weren't autistic, Black, or young.

Zs reject this filtered, hand-me-down storytelling. If you want to find out about autism, why ask Dustin Hoffman? Why not learn from someone on the spectrum?

That's the beauty of user-generated content, or UGC. The person whose story it is puts the content out themselves instead of someone else producing it and weakening its authenticity. No interference. No direction. No reductive stereotypes.

Of course, it's worth acknowledging the potential shortcomings of this approach. There's no mediation with UGC, true, but there's also no fact-checking or guarantee of authenticity. The *U* in UGC could stand for unregulated, unreliable, even untrue.

Yet Zs still push back on mainstream media content because it feels highly produced and stereotyped. During the BLM protests, they didn't turn to CNN or *The New York Times*. They used TikTok to watch posts from their Black peers talking directly about their experiences. At the same time, if they'd gone on Netflix, they would have found the network featuring *The Help*, a movie about a White Southerner's relationship with her Black maid. Zs do not see that as an authentic contribution to BLM.

Their storytelling bar is set way too high for that.

Authentic, multidimensional storytelling can literally save lives. The March 2021 shooting of six Asian women at a spa in Atlanta was directly motivated by the oversexualized stereotype perpetuated by the media. The shooter blamed Asian women for his sex addiction.

Zs are breaking down these reductive stereotypes by telling authentic stories. Ability is a good example. A Ford Foundation study found characters with different abilities (the term "disabled" is no longer universally accepted) were categorized into four stereotypes: the Super Crip, the Villain, the Victim, or the Innocent Fool. The study found that 22.9 percent of characters with disabilities in popular family films fit the Super Crip stereotype: the idea that a person with a disability needs to "overcome" their disability, which reinforces the superiority of people without disabilities (and thus, the importance of "overcoming" them). These portrayals flatten characters into a singular identity, their disability.

Nineteen-year-old Erin Novakowski is a creator with spinal muscular atrophy who describes her content as "me oversharing about being disabled—but doing it with super cute eyeliner on." In an interview for *Allure* magazine, she said, "I love getting a little *spicy* with my content and talking about embarrassing things like getting drunk or getting ghosted by boys, because abled people always assume disabled people don't experience normal things like that."

Social media stories allow for interactions impossible to achieve in previous generations. Zs' storytelling culture allows them to appreciate that everyone is different, while uniting them via shared exposure and empathy.

It's omniculturalism.

CULTURAL PRIDE

Inherent in the idea of omniculturalism is a celebration of the cultures within it. That's why we are seeing the reemergence of Zs embracing elements of their racial and ethnic heritage. Whereas previous generations downplayed distinct heritages, Zs' shared digital epicenter gives them access to other peers exploring similar racial and ethnic histories all over the world. A culture that might seem small or distant IRL feels accessible and intimate via the phone in their hand (in the same way Shina Novalinga has made Inuk culture accessible).

Virtually all studies around Generation We find increasing cultural pride among young Asian, Black, and Latinx in the United States. This is, however, happening in lockstep with an increase in Asian hate crime, systemic violence against the Black community, and attacks on Latin American immigration. Yet in the midst of negative prejudice, a look at TikTok reveals Z culture creating a space to celebrate what it means to be Asian, Black, or Latinx.

It's another example of Zs creating the world they wish to see—even if it only exists online.

In recent studies, 72 percent of Black Zs say they're proud of their heritage.[63] Likewise, 92 percent of Latinx feel that it's natural to live in the United States as an American yet still retain the culture of their country of origin.[64] Slightly more (95 per-

---

63 Tiffany Dorris, "America's Black Gen Z: Proud, Driven, and Changing the Narrative," ViacomCBS Global Insights, October 22, 2020, https://insights.viacomcbs.com/post/americas-black-gen-z-proud-driven-and-changing-the-narrative/.

64 Isaac Mizrahi, "Hispanic Millennials Are Closer to the Hispanic Culture than Most Think," *Forbes*, May 21, 2019, https://www.forbes.com/sites/isaacmizrahi/2019/05/20/hispanic-millennials-are-closer-to-the-hispanic-culture-than-most-think/?sh=272622136e63.

cent) believe it is important for future generations of Latinx in the United States to be able to speak Spanish.[65]

Online communities are being created intentionally to lift up populations that have historically been marginalized in the United States. #BlackGirlMagic was a hashtag coined in 2013 by CaShawn Thompson to celebrate the beauty, power, and resilience of Black women. While Thompson herself is not a Z, the hashtag launched a movement that young Black girls and women rallied around. In early 2021, 27 million users had posted images on Instagram celebrating the beauty and accomplishments of Black women.

You'll find online communities of Zs of different cultures exploring the foods, music, and traditions of their own culture and history, both in the United States and wherever their families originated. They share their newfound discoveries on social media, creating more broad-based interest in trying those foods or listening to that music. In this way, Zs go deeper into their own unique histories while simultaneously expanding their curiosity about and appreciation of others.

CULTURAL APPROPRIATION

But there's a flip side to omniculturalism, a phrase that can complicate the inherent optimism of its outlook: cultural appropriation. This refers to the use of elements of one culture by another, particularly the appropriation of a nondominant cultural element by a more dominant culture in a way that doesn't

---

65   Paul Taylor, Mark Hugo Lopez, Jessica Martínez, and Gabriel Velasco, "When Labels Don't Fit: Hispanics and Their Views of Identity," Pew Research Center, April 4, 2012, https://www.pewresearch.org/hispanic/2012/04/04/when-labels-dont-fit-hispanics-and-their-views-of-identity/.

respect the original meaning or that reinforces stereotypes or oppression. Like cancel culture, this has become a topic of intense media debate: when is a Halloween costume, a beauty trend, or the name a football team appropriate?

Generation We is quite clear on what is cultural appreciation versus cultural appropriation. But the difference is more difficult for older generation to grasp. They see a very fine line between what is and isn't okay. They wonder how they can identify the situations in which behavior that has been accepted throughout their lives—dressing up, sitting "Indian style," using words like "gypped" or "grandfathered in"—are suddenly deemed offensive.

Zs don't see the problem because they're far more likely to be fluent in the language of appropriation and to understand where a cultural reference comes from and how it's being used. For them, it's a question of accountability. It's about giving credit where it's due, which they see less as being overearnest and officious and more as simply being thoughtful about honoring and supporting a cultural group rather than using it to another group's benefit.

It is no surprise that the cultures that have been appropriated are mainly those that have been historically disadvantaged. When, for example, Victoria's Secret models are dressed in Native American headdresses and lingerie, it's not honoring Native American culture. It's superficial borrowing, because it looks cool on the runway. When White fraternities host "dress like a gangster" parties, sporting fake grills and carrying watermelons, it's not celebrating Black culture.

Zs argue that we should support disadvantaged cultures and lift them up, not just use their traditions for entertainment. It would be hard to find anyone who would disagree, but for those who aren't Zs, cultural appropriation relies on an education in authentic cultural history that frankly, older generations weren't necessary taught.

Gen Z are coining their own language to conduct the debate because the vocabulary otherwise available isn't up to the conversation. Take "Blackfishing," a term coined by journalist Wanna Thompson to describe the cultural appropriation of Black features by White women: dark tans, braided hairstyles, lip fillers, and emphasizing their thighs and butts. Zs have called out celebrities such as the Kardashians and Ariana Grande for co-opting the features and hairstyles of Black women, while actual Black women and men are still criminalized and punished for wearing their own natural hair. (As recently as 2018, a young girl in Louisiana was sent home from school because of her braided hairstyle; that same year, a high school student was forced to either cut his dreadlocks or forfeit his wrestling match: the video of him cutting his locks went viral.)

Or there's the "fox eye" trend, which is the appropriation of Asian features, specifically almond-shaped eyes. Fox eyes were a makeup craze in summer 2020—at precisely the same time Asian hate crime was rising in the United States due to COVID being labeled the "China virus" and blamed on East Asia. It's a particularly ambiguous set of values when celebrities are being praised online for the beauty of their artificially shaped eyes at the same time Asians are being attacked for having eyes that are naturally that shape.

TRUE REPRESENTATION

The conversation will continue because it is key to Zs' desire to acknowledge and fairly represent diversity. That representation is much broader than in the past because the diversity they recognize is much broader. Asian is not one box. There are millions of individual Asian stories in the United States, with many different cultural histories and lived experiences.

Zs expect to see an authentic range of diversity represented. They are tuned in and reject what they call tokenism—making a symbolic attempt to give the appearance of inclusion but superficially. Zs frequently call out tokenism in the media.

Just as "Asian" is not a single box, neither is "Black," or "Latinx," or "nonbinary." Gone are the days of casting one stereotypical character to check any of these boxes.

Zs have called out Hollywood for historically tending to cast Black actors with light skin (think Halle Berry or Denzel Washington). For Zs, it seems as if the people in power in Hollywood are afraid to cast somebody whose skin is too dark for fear that the audience won't find them as relatable. Two of the biggest Gen Z Black movie stars, Amandla Stenberg and Zendaya, freely acknowledge the advantages their relatively light skin has provided them in their careers. Zendaya said, "I have privilege compared to my darker sisters and brothers. And if I get put in a position because of the color of my skin, where people will listen to me, then I should use that privilege the right way."

Generation We demands true diversity of representation and representation of diversity. They want to move beyond the days of 2015 when a cisgender actor like Eddie Redmayne could play a trans woman in *The Danish Girl* (he was nominated for an Oscar for best actor). More recently, when Scarlett Johansson was cast to play an Asian protagonist, she lost the movie because of Z backlash, demanding that an Asian be hired to play the role.

There are those who counter that the whole point of acting is to pretend. For them, the logic that says that an actor should be Black to play Othello would also mean that only a Jewish actor could play Shylock—and taken to the extreme, that only a Dane could play Hamlet and a madman play King Lear.

Again, these are debates that will continue, and there will be missteps, as there will with the drive to define fictional characters more as individuals than stereotypes. Bernadette Beck, a Black, bisexual actor on the TV show *Riverdale* went so far as to complain about her own character, saying, "I feel like I'm just there to fill a diversity quota...And because I'm bisexual, they cast me as this tough bruiser kind of girl." She was one of four Black Gen Z actors on the CW network, which is very popular with Zs, who publicly challenged the racist, sexist, and homophobic stereotypes on the network's superhero shows.

As Beck observed, "Long term, if we're depicted as unlikable or the enemy all the time, that affects public perception."

Media and entertainment companies are heeding Z demands because Zs are among their most elusive audiences and potentially one of the most lucrative. As we'll see in Chapter 9, Zs may become the richest generation in the country, and they're ruthless consumers, because the internet gives them so many options for entertainment. So networks will increasingly bring diversity into homes across the country, whether invited or not.

This transition is evident in how the Disney Channel translated the original 2006 movie *High School Musical*, about high school thespians, singers, and dancers, into a weekly TV series in 2019. Unlike the original movie, Disney intentionally cast a diverse range of body types. The size of the multiple plus-sized characters—all great singers and dancers—is never mentioned in the storyline. Their size is not integral to the story or their character development. One of the actresses said, "Everywhere I look, there is beauty in so many colors and shapes and sizes...I know how important it is to feel represented in the media because growing up, I didn't feel that I had that."

At the end of 2020, the UCLA Center for Storytelling analyzed 109 movies from the previous five years and concluded that bringing authentic diversity to film, as in, say, the *Black Panther* movie or Pixars's *Coco*, is profitable. It found that a studio can expect to lose up to $130 million on a film that lacks authentic diversity.

Authenticity is key. Consider Disney's evolution from how it represented past protagonists (like *Pocahontas* in 1995 or *Mulan* in 1998) to *Moana* in 2016, where an "Oceanic Trust" of anthropologists, cultural practitioners, historians, linguists, and choreographers from Samoa, Tahiti, Mo'orea, and Fiji were integral in shaping details from character design to song lyrics.

It is worth noting that although *Moana* was unprecedented for Disney in terms of cultural authenticity, it was still directed by four White men. Zs are elevating the discussion around who has the rights to tell a story and deciding that it's often not a White male filmmaker...So it seems inevitable that we will see a more diverse range of Z creators and storytellers rise up to create the narratives of this generation.

DIVERSITY AT WORK

It's not just the media. Zs have also called out representation in corporate leadership on the same grounds. Making a percentage of diverse hires is one thing, but if a corporation does not have diversity at the top, in the boardroom, it's not real representation. When a Z on TikTok looked at the *Fortune* 100 CEOs, he found only eight women and no women of color; there were three Hispanic men, three Black men, and five Asian men. Of the eighty-odd White male CEOs, there were more CEOs named Michael (eight), James (seven), or David (seven) than there were Black and Hispanic CEOs put together.

This is real for Zs, given their demographics. More than two-thirds of Zs (68 percent) say they have decided not to apply for a job for fear of workplace discrimination. About two-thirds said they had witnessed discrimination in the workplace based on race, ethnicity, gender identity, or sexual orientation.[66]

To go back to one of the most notorious Z contributions: gender pronouns. Some 88 percent of Zs believe recruiters or employers should ask their preferred gender pronouns when they are being recruited or interviewed.[67] A quarter said they would decline a job offer if an employer failed to use their preferred pronouns. Of course, many Zs aren't in the job market yet, so for them this is purely hypothetical, but simply making the claim shows how important this is to them. (And imagine how you might feel if your employer consistently referred to you as "she" when you're a he, or vice versa. Anyone would think about walking out.)

The fact is that within a couple of years, whenever anyone goes

---

66 "The Survey Is In: Gen Z Demands Diversity and Inclusion Strategy," Tallo, October 21, 2020, https://tallo.com/blog/genz-demands-diversity-inclusion-strategy/.

67 Ibid.

for an interview, they will be asked about their pronoun preference as a matter of course.

Zs are demanding that corporations reflect true representation in their communication as never before—and they're getting it. Victoria's Secret and Aerie are two underwear companies with contrasting stories. Zs have been fleeing Victoria's Secret for a while. It has been villainized for multiple transgressions, including cultural appropriation and a failure to represent body and gender diversity. In 2019, CEO Lex Wexner felt the need to respond to the criticism. To say he got it wrong would be an understatement.

Not only did Wexner refuse to portray a wider range of shapes, sizes, and gender on the runway, but he said that to do so would spoil the fantasies of the men he saw as his core market. When public pressure continued, he simply announced that Victoria's Secret would do no more runway shows.

The stock fell 41 percent that year, and Wexner was forced to quit.

In contrast, Aerie, American Eagle's underwear line, is hugely body positive. It represents all kinds of body diversity in its advertising, including trans models and a range of abilities. For several years, Aerie has publicly banned all photo retouching of their models and increasingly featured UGC of real customers with real bodies wearing their underwear. As of the writing of this book, it has now posted eighteen consecutive quarters of double-digit growth.

DESCRIPTIVE REPRESENTATION

In politics, Zs clearly see that the US government is less

diverse than the population it serves. There has been a 50 percent increase in the number of women in Congress in the last decade—now constituting 27 percent of the 117th Congress—but the population is 51 percent women.[68] It's progress, sure, but only halfway, and far fewer of these women are BIPOC. In January 2021, when Raphael Warnock was celebrated as the first Democratic senator ever elected in a Southern state, he was still one of only three Black senators in the 117th Congress.

A lot of Zs get their politics from an unexpected source: *Teen Vogue*. Its political desk does a remarkable job writing about things from Gen Z's perspective. When *The New York Times* hailed the diversity of Joe Biden's first cabinet, *Teen Vogue* criticized it for being only superficially diverse. (In March 2021, incidentally, *Teen Vogue* itself fell victim to the perils of leading the conversation about accountability culture when its editor, Alexi McCammond, a young Z woman, was ousted for tweets she had sent when younger.)

Superficial diversity is one of Zs' most acute concerns. It focuses on identity markers, such as skin color, racial identity, ethnicity, or religion, versus substantive representation, which is about a person substantively representing diverse populations in their policies and actions.

The starting point is that not all representation is the same. For example, Ruth Bader Ginsburg was replaced on the US Supreme Court by another woman, Amy Coney Barrett. But RBG was a huge proponent of women's rights, and Barrett is not. Her representation of women is unlikely to be the same.

---

68   Carrie Blazina and Drew DeSilver, "A Record Number of Women Are Serving in the 117th Congress," Pew Research Center, January 22, 2021, https://www.pewresearch.org/fact-tank/2021/01/15/a-record-number-of-women-are-serving-in-the-117th-congress/.

Or contrast Thurgood Marshall, the first Black Justice on the Supreme Court, longtime civil rights litigator for the NAACP, including *Brown v. Board of Education* (declaring segregated schools unconstitutional), with the contemporary Black Justice Clarence Thomas, who is the most right-leaning Justice on the court and makes no exception for BIPOC.

Zs say you need to look beyond simply appointing women and non-Whites: you have to look at a politician's record and who is really supporting diversity. It has to go more than skin deep. Most recently, Zs noted the significance of Kamala Harris becoming vice-president because she's a Black, South Asian woman, for example, but they were also critical of her mixed record on policing, incarceration, and transgender rights.

As with society in general, a portion of Zs fear diversity. Research suggests they're a small percentage of the generation, but we saw young faces storming the Capitol in January 2021. We know a subset are active in groups like the Proud Boys and cling powerfully to deep-seated white supremacist beliefs. We know these Zs are just as savvy at using social media to mobilize and organize as their more liberal peers, and much has been written about the far-right radicalization of teens on YouTube and in spaces on the dark web. In 2019, the Anti-Defamation League reported an increase in white supremacist recruitment on college campuses for the third year in a row, with 313 cases being reported. The fear of change, even in the name of diversity, has brought groups like this out of the background and into the Twitter feeds of Zs.[69]

---

69 Caitlin Gibson, "'Do You Have White Teenage Sons? Listen Up.' How White Supremacists Are Recruiting Boys Online," *The Washington Post*, September 17, 2019, https://www.washingtonpost.com/lifestyle/on-parenting/do-you-have-white-teenage-sons-listen-up-how-white-supremacists-are-recruiting-boys-online/2019/09/17/f081e806-d3d5-11e9-9343-40db57cf6abd_story.html.

FLEXING OUR SUPERPOWER

The majority of Generation We is challenging the United States' historical relationship with diversity, seeing diversity not as something to be feared or something to be accommodated but as something to be celebrated. Zs use their platforms to build awareness and equity across a breadth of diverse populations, especially those that were historically marginalized.

That advocacy is showing up in unexpected places, such as the Arthur Ashe Stadium at Flushing Meadows, New York. At the height of the BLM movement in summer 2020, Z tennis player Naomi Osaka wore a different black mask at each of her seven matches in the US Open tournament, each displaying the name of a victim of police injustice: Ahmaud Arbery, Philando Castile, George Floyd, Trayvon Martin, Elijah McClain, Tamir Rice, and Breonna Taylor. Talk about using your platform.

Immigration is highly relevant to Zs, as many of them are Dreamers, children of illegal immigrants raised in the United States and offered a chance to stay by Obama-era legislation. The majority—two-thirds—of DACA recipients are Zs under twenty-five years old.[70] During the Trump administration, Dreamers in US classrooms didn't have to worry only about homework assignments or getting to sports practice on time; they also had to follow news on the government's efforts to have them deported—in some cases to countries they had never even visited. Who can blame them if they question the system?

Dreamers shared their stories online with the result that, as a generation, Zs became educated on US immigration policy. They

---

70 Gustavo López and Jens Manuel Krogstad, "Key Facts about 'Dreamers' Enrolled in DACA," Pew Research Center, May 30, 2020, https://www.pewresearch.org/fact-tank/2017/09/25/key-facts-about-unauthorized-immigrants-enrolled-in-daca/.

learned that the system hadn't always criminalized immigrants. They learned that Immigration and Customs Enforcement (ICE) didn't even exist until about twenty years ago. Immigration police didn't used to roam the streets. There were immigration issues, yes, but immigration was not a crime. The system of mass policing, detention, and deportation is recent. Zs, believing our nation is stronger for its diversity of people, experiences, and perspectives, are looking to decriminalize the whole immigration system, making the entire United States a sanctuary country.

As we have seen, Zs are passionate about telling unique and authentic stories. And that includes telling authentic stories retroactively. That means looking back at our history with clear eyes and removing all of the whitewashing that was passed along to older generations. It means reading schoolbooks that not only acknowledge wrongdoings and expose systemic prejudices in the past but that also celebrate the important role of Black and Chinese and Indigenous and Mexican and every other population in the creation of our country. It means calling Thanksgiving Indigenous Peoples' Day, a process already well underway in our schools. It means elevating the significance of Juneteenth—the day we celebrate the emancipation of slaves. (Although Donald Trump claimed to have popularized the holiday after being forced to reschedule an event for Juneteenth, he certainly didn't introduce the day of recognition to many Zs.)

Generation We are not afraid of exposing the truths in our history and in our present. They are not afraid of the hard conversations. They are having those conversations every day online, across geography, across race, across ethnicity, across gender, and across every other amalgam of identity. Through this process, they are defining their own rich identities in the way every teenager does—but they are doing it while building a wiser, stronger, more empathetic, and united culture than ever before.

To achieve that, however, they first have to secure the planet's future.

Z Voices

ERIN NOVAKOWSKI: THE STORYTELLER

Nineteen-year-old Erin Novakowski (she/they) is a content creator (@wheelierin) with a fast-growing following, a disability advocate, and a writer/editor for youth-led Cripple Media.

Q: Tell me a little bit about your story.

A: I was born with spinal muscular atrophy, type two. It's a genetic disorder that affects all the muscles in my body, which basically become weaker over time. I've been in a power wheelchair for most of my life; my wheelchair is a big part of my identity. My disability is a big part of my identity. As I grew up, I started to learn that if I didn't advocate for myself very loudly and very clearly, I wouldn't get what I needed or do what I wanted to do in my life. That was very apparent, not only in school but in everyday life, in accessibility. So I just learned to be very loud about things.

The internet gave me a place to let more people hear me be loud, I guess. I don't consider myself an activist or anything, but I really like telling my story. I'm very happy to overshare. I'm constantly posting every thought that enters my mind, but that's going to translate into letting people know my experiences and I hope that it helps them understand.

Q: There are a lot of different and evolving languages surrounding disabilities. Can you talk about the language you prefer to use?

A: Since I've been on TikTok, random people will feel compelled to tell me that I'm not disabled, that I am "specially abled" or "handicapable" or whatever fun word they've come up with that week to just ignore the fact that I'm disabled. And the thing is, I am disabled; I identify as disabled. I'm sitting in a 300-pound wheelchair that has been with me for nineteen years and that's part of who I am. So when people try to dance around the subject or tell me that I am just like them, it's just not true. I'm not ashamed of being disabled. I'm very proud of my identity. I love being disabled and I love my community. So it's just incredibly frustrating when nondisabled people try to tell me who I am or what I'm not.

Q: We have been talking about the difference between diversity and tokenism a lot. Do you have thoughts on the differences between these and what they mean to you?

A: Diversity is more who I see. Like on television, I don't see myself. Now that I've found a community online, I do get to see myself. But as a child, when I was struggling the most with the way that my body looked or how my body worked or whatever, there was no diversity in terms of who was famous on social media, who was on television, who was in fashion. That affected me a lot. Tokenism is why I am incredibly loud. I'm very loud with my ideas because people can and often do see disabled people and say, "She's so inspiring. Look at her. She made a joke about her disability. That's amazing." And that's not what I want because me making a stupid joke on TikTok is not inspiring. I am not an inspiring person just for existing and doing things I like. When I am just sitting here in my silly little room doing my silly little internet things.

Q: Why is it so important for marginalized groups to control their own narrative?

A: When I was younger, most of the content portrayed disabled people like a burden, which is something that I've struggled with my whole life. That whole narrative is super harmful to any disabled people who consume it. When you don't center on their experiences, if you're not actually including and listening to the person that you're trying to speak, write, or make a film about, then whatever you say is just incorrect to some degree.

Q: Tell us about the community you're a part of online.

A: The editor in chief of Cripple Media and another friend and I talk every day. I consider them my best friends. We're all in wheelchairs; we're all in Cripple Media. We are the same person in three different fonts and we know what each other is going through. We can talk about literally anything. And there's no judgment. There's no confusion because we can talk about cripple things and we all just know what's happening. And then I've learned so much on TikTok. As soon as I started getting support from other disabled TikTokers, I thought, "This is the coolest place on the internet; I'm never leaving." It's amazing how making a sixty-second video, and the right person finding it, we can become so close. It would not be possible if the internet didn't exist.

Q: Imagine your vision for the world is enacted, the world according to Erin: what would that look like?

A: I like to joke with my other disabled friends that sometimes we are so angry because of everything that we could literally take over the world if we wanted to. Our community is so strong and we're able to support each other through the internet. So many systems are built to just let disabled people die because it's expensive to be disabled and it's stressful to be disabled. When you have resources from other people who are living it and surviving it, you can survive anything.

CHAPTER 8

Climate Generation

"There's only so much the average human can do in their daily lives to combat climate change. Recycling and reducing our use of gas/oil can help only so much. Big companies that make millions while continuously straining the earth's natural resources and causing pollution need to take from profits to fix their carbon footprint."

—TWENTY-YEAR-OLD Z, LOUISIANA

It's no surprise that Generation We believes climate is the most serious issue facing them today. Previous generations treated the climate crisis like a hypothetical future. They contemplated it with the luxury of time, like passengers worrying about the arrangement of deckchairs on the *Titanic* because the iceberg was still over the horizon.

For Zs, the crisis arrived on the planet before they did. They were born into the middle of it. The six years leading up to 2021 were the six hottest on record.

They truly are the Climate Generation.

Zs have grown up learning about climate models in school that track pivotal climate benchmarks in eerie lockstep with milestones in their lives. The IPCC (the UN Intergovernmental Panel on Climate Change) projects the rise in the temperature of Earth's climate could exceed 1.5°C above preindustrial levels, a key marker for increased ecological and social instability, as early as 2030 if the current trajectory does not change.[71] Zs will be between twenty and thirty-three years old, still living on college campuses, beginning their careers, or contemplating starting a family.

If the climate emergency feels more personal to Generation We, that's because it is. Which is why they won't accept any more time wasted.

They can *see* the damn iceberg, and they know we've already made contact. They know once the front of the ship takes on too much water, it will be hard to avoid sinking.

THIS IS HAPPENING

The longest-range climate models only go through 2100. That means the youngest Zs will actually *outlive* our current climate projections. No more hypotheticals. Their whole lives will be defined by the climate trajectory: the natural resources they can use, the natural disasters they will suffer, the climate migration and resource scarcity that will test the global balance of power and the structures of government, the political and social instability that could follow.

Zs don't have the luxury of kicking the can down the road.

---

71   "IPCC, 2018: Summary for Policymakers," in *Global Warming of 1.5°C* (Geneva: World Meteorological Organization, 2018).

That is why Generation We is co-opting the climate movement. In an Amnesty International survey, more than 10,000 Zs across twenty-two countries rated climate change the most important issue facing the world.

That's because they're living it.

In 2020, there were so many hurricanes in the United States that scientists ran out of letters to name them and had to start using Greek letters. Five of California's six largest wildfires in history burned in 2020, and the two largest fires ever in Colorado. Phoenix, Arizona, set a record of 144 days when the temperature topped 100°F.[72] The same year set a new record, with twenty-two climate disasters in the United States that each cost over $1 billion. Since 2000, the country has experienced 208 billion-dollar climate events at a total cost of $1.449 trillion. Oh, and nearly 10,000 lives lost.[73] That's the cost of not acting.

Zs grew up with natural disasters the norm. Kids in the Southwest stay in their classrooms when it's too hot to go outside for recess. During fire season, kids in parts of California and Colorado keep their prized possessions in the car ready to evacuate at a moment's notice. Kids in coastal areas watch their parents prepare their homes for floods, batten down the windows, and know where the family's survival kit is kept. These homes, once a safe haven of childhood, are in the climate's direct line of fire. Parents teach their kids about the impermanence of physical structures so they'll be prepared if disaster strikes and they have

72 Ian Livingston, "Phoenix Has Hit 100 Degrees on Record-Breaking Half of the Days in 2020," *The Washington Post*, October 15, 2020, https://www.washingtonpost.com/weather/2020/10/14/phoenix-record-heat-100-degrees/?utm_campaign=wp_main&utm_source=twitter&utm_medium=social&utm_source=reddit.com.

73 "Billion-Dollar Weather and Climate Disasters: Overview," National Climatic Data Center, 2021, https://www.ncdc.noaa.gov/billions/.

to return after tropical storms or wildfires to gutted homes and schools. Being a climate refugee does not only happen in distant lands; an increasing number of families in the United States are only one weather event away.

CLIMATE ANXIETY

For Zs, climate has always been a part of their reality. The majority say climate change has already impacted where they live and how they think about their future.[74] A sixteen-year-old from California told us, "Wildfires have become normal. Just forty miles away, thousands of homes burned down. Air quality is terrible on fire days. Instead of snow days, California now has smoke days." A twenty-one-year-old in Texas explained, "The heat rises every year, with temperatures that can reach 120°. This past winter, a freeze took over Texas and caused the air temp to reach –5° where I live. This had a disastrous effect on wildlife. All across the Gulf, there were billions of dead fish and sea life found on the shores." And a twenty-two-year-old in Florida said, "Living on the coast, the potential for sea level rise threatens my home and the rise in temperature threatens the sea turtle populations in my oceans. Sea turtles whose gender depends on the temperature of the sand during their incubation period are mostly being born female as temperatures continue to rise."

And we're currently at only about 1.0°C above preindustrial levels.

What's all the fuss about 1.5°C? The science says that with a rise of 1.5°C, one-sixth of Earth's population will experience severe

---

74   Research by ZSpeak by Global Mosaic, May 2021.

heat waves and drought, making large areas uninhabitable, while other swaths of the planet receive extreme precipitation, flooding, and tropical storms. A percentage of insects, vertebrates, and plants will die as entire ecosystems transform; polar ice sheets will melt, raising sea levels across coastlines; oceans will increase in acidity, creating "dead zones" without fish, while coral reefs will decline by 70–90 percent.[75]

On our current trajectory, we could zip past 1.5°C in the next decade and be well on our way to 2°C by mid-century, and 3°C+ by 2100, at which point the situation becomes that much more dire. Older generations weren't taught this. The science didn't exist for most of us. Zs, on the other hand, have been learning about it since kindergarten.

Listen to the science, they plead with the rest of us.

The mid-century mark, 2050, is when the Paris Agreement says we must hit net-zero carbon emissions to stop temperatures from rising further. Less than thirty years out, we are not on track to hit the target, and Zs know this. When we asked them what they thought our world would be like in 2050, a twenty-three-year-old from South Carolina said, "Sea levels will rise to the point that major cities will have to be evacuated. People will have to start moving inland." Another twenty-three-year-old from Maine added, "Many places in the world will be uninhabitable. Population densities in certain areas will explode. There will be conflicts resulting from diminishing resources. All this will dramatically increase economic inequality."

These are kids in their early twenties contemplating their own

---

75 "Global Warming of 1.5 ºC," Intergovernmental Panel on Climate Change, 2021.

middle-aged lives. They hear the Secretary General of the United Nations saying that climate change is an existential threat to the future of humanity, and they feel as if he's speaking directly to them.

Zs have the lowest stated intention of having children of any generation that has preceded them, partly because of their concerns around the uncertain future of the planet. One seventeen-year-old in Missouri said, "Climate change has affected my decisions on where I'd like to live in the future, colleges I want to attend, and has made me have doubts about future children." Meanwhile, a twenty-three-year-old in Pennsylvania contemplates, "It impacts whether or not I want kids because I don't want to bring children into a world where they might suffer."

That's how heavily it weighs on Zs: that potentially the greatest gift they can give their children is simply for them not to be born. Parents who have been looking forward to grandchildren heed this. As Gina McCarthy, who became National Climate Advisor when Joe Biden became president in 2021, said, "The world is changing. The reason why we're seeing people my age on the streets is probably because we were given the gift of having grandchildren. I'm not now worried about my sacrifice. I'm worried about handing to them a future that I'm going to be proud of."

There's so much evidence that it's hard to process. Older generations have noted that Greta Thunberg and other youth climate activists seem so angry as they ask the world, "How dare you?" and accuse older generations of "stealing" their future.

A lot of the anger comes from fear. Zs know the science and feel traumatized because they're trapped in the middle of the story.

Jamie Margolin, who co-founded the youth climate organization Zero Hour and testified in front of Congress with Greta Thunberg, has been very public about the relationship between activism and mental health, and the brief shelf life a lot of young activists experience. In an interview with The Alliance for Climate Education, she said, "We are taught all about the actions people need to take, but we hardly ever talk about the toll those actions take on people. It is easy in today's hustle culture to get so caught up in the 'doing' aspect of activism that you forget how it feels and end up burning yourself out."

This feeling has a diagnosable name. The American Psychological Association (APA) has created an entirely new vocabulary to diagnose the disorders from which Zs suffer: climate anxiety, eco grief, climate-induced PTSD.

Can we blame Zs, when by definition an existential threat means the climate is a threat to their very existence? Sarah Ray, a professor who teaches environmental studies, warned about the effects she sees in her own students because her course has become a catalog of threats to their future. "Some students become so overwhelmed with despair and grief that they shut down. Many stop coming to lectures and seminars. They send depressed, despairing emails. They lose their bearings, question their relationships and education, and barely pass their classes."

One of her students developed such self-loathing that the only way the student could think to reduce her own environmental impact was to stop consuming entirely. She started starving herself. Most Zs take a less apocalyptic approach. But they are all impacted.

FROM INDIVIDUAL TO COLLECTIVE RESPONSIBILITY

There's a misperception among older generations that Zs don't really understand the issues about climate change, that they're mainly interested in tangential interests, flaunting their metal straws and "Save the Turtle" water bottle stickers. Or that they are just disgruntled youth lamenting the failure of older generations, as all young generations lament their elders.

In reality, Zs' understanding is sophisticated and the whole generation is solution-oriented.

Zs understand that the core issue is carbon emissions and who's creating them. And Gen Z sees that means the issue is really about power: who has the power to release carbon and who has the power to stop it. They know this power is deeply entrenched in our systems and that the actors that run these systems have historically had a vested interest in the status quo: the banks, the corporations, the energy companies, the governments. That's a lot for teenagers to take on.

As a Gen Xer, I was taught that looking after the environment was an individual responsibility. We didn't litter and we had service days when we'd go out and pick up other people's litter. The next generation, the millennials, were taught to recycle, again placing responsibility on the individual.

The savvy Zs have redirected the conversation from individual to collective responsibility. Of course, Generation We takes personal actions to reduce environmental impact. But they know that what is really required to reduce CO_2 emissions is change within corporations and governments and within infrastructure and energy systems. It will take the whole of the private and public sectors to turn this ship and avoid sinking. And Zs are relentless in demanding immediate action from both.

Climate facts go viral on TikTok and YouTube as Zs spread information, like the fact that one hundred companies are responsible for 71 percent of all global emissions,[76] or that there are so many microplastics in our ecosystem that we each eat a credit card's worth of plastic every week.[77] So, while they're tossing their milk cartons into the correct recycling bin, they're also asking themselves how companies are still allowed to burn fossil fuels and pollute with impunity.

They know. Individual acts are no longer enough.

IT'S ALL INTERSECTIONAL

Climate is the ultimate intersectional issue—and as we know, no one is more aware of intersectionality than Zs. Youth-led climate movements educate their members on the systemic roots of the climate crisis, including colonialism and extractive capitalism, and its connections with race, geography, and socioeconomic inequality. When these movements call for a "just transition" to a carbon-neutral economy, they are recognizing that the marginalized, frontline communities on islands and coasts, and BIPOC, who are disproportionally affected by climate change are often also the very communities that depend on fossil fuel jobs.

Zs also know this disparity was not an accident but part of

---

76 Tess Riley, "100 Companies Are Responsible for 71% of Global Emissions, Study Says," Business & Human Rights Resource Centre, July 10, 2017, https://www.business-humanrights.org/en/latest-news/100-companies-are-responsible-for-71-of-global-emissions-study-says/.

77 "No Plastic in Nature: Assessing Plastic Ingestion from Nature to People," World Wildlife Fund for Nature, 2019, https://awsassets.panda.org/downloads/plastic_ingestion_press_singles.pdf.

a system that deprioritized the interests of BIPOC and low-income communities. From pipelines through Indigenous lands to poisoned water in Flint, Michigan, environmental racism is real. Although the environment itself has no agenda, companies and governments have historically placed plants, pipelines, toxic waste facilities, and garbage dumps near marginalized communities with less power. Seven years into Flint's water crisis, residents still did not have access to clean drinking water. It's hard to imagine a White suburb where the problem would still not have been solved.

Zs acknowledge that you can't just take fossil fuel jobs away. Saving the planet at the expense of ruining communities or leaving families hungry isn't justice. On the flip side, the longer it takes to build new infrastructure, train, and transition these communities to jobs in a new renewable economy, the more island and coastline communities will sink. That isn't justice either.

So Zs are asking for everything. They want a just transition, but they also want it to happen right now. Certainly, this will require a delicate balance. What is clear is that their relentless, ambitious demands and refusal to compromise have created momentum, and recent policies and climate commitments are pushing further and faster than ever before.

A HUMAN PROBLEM

Zs are also influencing a change in how we view the concept of climate. To them, it's less an environmental problem than a human problem. To older generations, global warming connoted chemical compounds floating in the atmosphere. Zs see that it's all about human suffering. The difference between 1.5°C and 2°C is hundreds of millions of humans displaced, significant loss of life, and the disappearance of entire island nations.

Generation We have a sophisticated approach to language and its power. They rarely use the words "climate change" because they believe the phrase makes what is happening sound more benign than it is. Instead, they call it the climate *crisis*, climate *emergency*, or climate *revolution*.

Increasingly, they call their work climate *justice* because that reflects how it affects humans. Rather than climate migration, they specifically talk about climate *refugees*, drawing a parallel between the climate emergency and the suffering experienced during wartime.

It's a whole shift in language.

Their intention is to ask us, how much human suffering are we willing to accept?

WHAT ZS WANT

Greta Thunberg started taking Fridays off school in Stockholm, Sweden, in 2018. She started Fridays for Future so that every Friday kids around the world would walk out of school to bring awareness to the climate emergency.

For many people, that was their most enduring image of climate protests. Kids walking out of school and teachers and administrators encouraging or applauding them for doing so. Today, the movement has gone way beyond that.

Greta may be the only household name, but she is just one of millions of Zs who are mobilizing around climate. The three most active climate organizations in the United States are all youth led: Fridays for Future was started by Greta in Sweden and has millions of American followers; Zero Hour, co-founded by Jamie Margolin with Zanagee Artis in Seattle when Margolin was just fifteen, now boasts forty-two sister chapters internationally; and the Sunrise Movement, founded by several friends on the East Coast in 2015, has more than 400 hubs and chapters around the world. The growth of these organizations speaks to the tremendous power and voice they increasingly wield.

Despite the daunting challenges, Generation We is working tirelessly to make change. When we asked, more than two-thirds of Zs around the United States agreed that "we have the collective power to make an impact on climate."[78] Their behavior demonstrates this.

Although older generations are still the ones running the corporations and governments, the United Nations, and other governing bodies, Zs have become very effective at exerting pressure for change. Their fingerprints are all over everything connected to climate. All three youth-led organizations are now at the forefront of our biggest climate discussions.

They all executed huge voter turnout efforts in advance of the 2020 elections, with thousands of Zs conducting outreach via email, text, and phone. Sunrise alone contacted more than 6.5 million young voters.[79] Zero Hour co-founder Zanagee Artis not only led their #Vote4ourFuture initiative but became a fellow for Joe Biden's campaign. These organizations understood the

---

78 Research by ZSpeak by Global Mosaic, May 2021.

79 "Our Success by the Numbers: Sunrise Movement Election Impact," Sunrise Movement, November 11, 2020, https://www.sunrisemovement.org/our-election-impact/.

importance of campaigning at the state level too, partnering with grassroots organizations to attempt to swing important seats that would allow for a climate-friendly House and Senate and to support specific candidates who supported the Green New Deal.

Joe Biden was not Zs' first choice as president, but their mobilization speaks to their pragmatism. They could see that he was their best chance. And as we've seen, youth showed up to vote in record numbers—the largest youth vote in history. In a post-election poll conducted by *The New York Times*, 90 percent of Biden voters said they were concerned about their community being harmed by climate change; only 23 percent of Trump voters said the same.[80] Biden was clearly the candidate if you cared about climate.

Pre-election, none of the Z climate organizations thought Biden's ideas went far enough, mostly because he never endorsed the Green New Deal. Post-election, Zs were quick to take credit: we all showed up to vote, we gave you a climate mandate, now act on it. They immediately turned up the heat, making demands of the new administration. Sunrise organized nationwide youth rallies the day after Biden's inauguration, on January 21, 2021, to hold him accountable. Their website declared, "Democrats have no more excuses. No Republican Senate blocking them, no Trump White House. The time for excuses is over. Now's the time for Democrats to deliver and it's on us to make them. There's nobody else coming. We can't pass this off to the next generation as prior generations did to us. It's on us to act now to fight for the future we believe in. We must be the ones we've been waiting for."

---

80 Brad Plumer and Nadja Popovich, "What Voters in Battleground States Think about Climate Change," *The New York Times*, November 1, 2020, https://www.nytimes.com/interactive/2020/11/01/climate/polls-what-voters-think-climate-global-warming.html.

Although Biden has not gone as far as embracing the Green New Deal (which is Zs' gold standard), his actions on climate were ambitious and worked toward many of their demands. Creating climate mandates within each agency spoke to the administration's commitment to intersectionality. Biden's $2 trillion infrastructure plan aimed to transition the United States into a modern, climate-resilient economy, while creating millions of new "clean" jobs and specifically addressing social and economic inequities. He moved quickly to invest in electric cars, with half a million chargers by 2030, a 100 percent green energy grid by 2035, and a net-zero economy by 2050. Biden's plan also included ideas Z organizations had been promoting, like a Civilian Climate Corps that employs people to conserve public lands. Biden's climate goals were big and unprecedented. As Biden said, "It is a once-in-a-generation investment in America."

The Green New Deal has ten key demands, some of which are specific to climate but many of which are not. Some are reminiscent of the old New Deal, like guaranteeing a federal job and universal healthcare to every American. Again, Zs are relentlessly ambitious and uncompromising. Some might say this is inspiring, while others might say it is unrealistic. This much is certain: Generation We will continue to push the goalposts forward.

MOCK MEETING

In 2015, the United Nations annual climate conference, the Conference of the Parties (COP) 21, created the Paris Agreement to set targets for the world's countries to reduce their carbon emissions. The youngest Zs were just five at the time. But they've studied the Paris Agreement and what it means throughout their school careers. And what they've learned is this: the original carbon emission commitments in the Paris Agreement fell far short of what's actually needed. The goal set in Paris was to keep temperature increase well below 2°C, while pursuing efforts of achieving 1.5°C. The original commitments from 2015 put us more on track for 3°C+.

Part of the reason for the disparity is updated science and modeling since 2015. Part is that the COP is a political body requiring voluntary commitments from each country and that the agreement takes a bottom-up approach, stipulating that every country raise their carbon-cutting goals every five years. The original commitments were always meant to be the floor, not the ceiling.

What was spectacularly significant about the Paris Agreement was that it was the first truly global commitment to fight the climate crisis: 195 countries signing on, acknowledging the importance of collective action. Even at the time, participating countries knew the original commitments weren't enough. The upping of each country's goals was scheduled for COP 26 in Glasgow in 2020.

The latest science from the IPCC in advance of COP 26 said the only way we have a reasonable chance to hit the 1.5°C target is to cut total global emissions in half by the end of 2030 and to reach net-zero by 2050.[81] Given this, Generation We were anxious to see the revised targets.

Then COVID happened, and COP 26 was canceled: it was postponed an entire year, until November 2021. Zs were very

---

81 "Summary for Policymakers of IPCC Special Report on Global Warming of 1.5°C Approved by Governments," IPCC, October 8, 2018, https://www.ipcc.ch/2018/10/08/summary-for-policymakers-of-ipcc-special-report-on-global-warming-of-1-5c-approved-by-governments/.

unhappy. The planet is in the middle of an environmental crisis, and yet the world's political leaders all stayed home.

Gen Z would not accept inaction. They created their own Mock COP 26, a full two-week online global climate conference run by young climate activists. More than 330 delegates from eleven years old through their twenties represented more than 140 countries around the world. Because the Southern Hemisphere usually lacks the same representation as the north, they made sure that 72 percent of delegates came from the south. At the end of two weeks, the delegates signed a global declaration with eighteen policies directed at the adults who would attend the rescheduled real COP 26 in 2021, signed from "The Youth of the World."

No more time for inaction.

THE KIDS JUST KEEP SHOWING UP

As with their Mock COP 26, the kids just keep showing up.

Generation We is about taking action because Zs understand they have become a formidable power bloc. And they're using every tool at their disposal. To quote the Sunrise Movement website again: "We were born into crisis. We inherited a failing world. We tried signing petitions. We tried calling and visiting government offices. Through it all, most politicians ignored us. Now we're taking actions they cannot ignore. Our generation is done asking."

They point to encounters with politicians like Democratic Senator Dianne Feinstein of California in 2019, when a group of Zs, one as young as seven, went to her office to seek support for the

Green New Deal. After telling them she didn't support it, she then said (in a video recorded by Sunrise), "I've been doing this for thirty years...I've gotten elected. I just ran. I was elected by almost a million-vote plurality. And I know what I'm doing. So you know, maybe people should listen a little bit."[82]

So Zs resort to other tactics.

In the past two years, Zs have launched lawsuits against the US government, as well as legal actions against six individual states. Seven Zs in Florida are suing the state for not upholding the Public Trust Doctrine, protecting their land, water, and atmosphere. In *Juliana v. United States*, twenty-one Zs are suing the federal government for violation of their generation's constitutional rights to life, liberty, and prosperity and for failure to protect essential public trust resources.[83]

In a huge win for Zs, in April 2021 Germany's top court rejected the country's climate plan for not being ambitious enough and placing too much burden on future generations to reduce carbon emissions. The court said the government plan was "not sufficient to ensure that the necessary transition to climate neutrality is achieved in time." Germany's Friday for Future chapter tweeted, "Today, the German constitutional court has decided that climate justice is a fundamental right. Today's inaction mustn't harm our freedom and rights in the future."[84]

---

82 Bill McKibben, "The Hard Lessons of Dianne Feinstein's Encounter with the Young Green New Deal Activists," *The New Yorker*, February 23, 2019, https://www.newyorker.com/news/daily-comment/the-hard-lessons-of-dianne-feinsteins-encounter-with-the-young-green-new-deal-activists-video.

83 "Securing the Legal Right to a Safe Climate," Our Children's Trust, 2021.

84 Guy Chazan, "Constitutional Court Strikes Down German Climate Law," *Financial Times*, April 29, 2021, https://www.ft.com/content/6be3ea51-653d-47c2-8ef9-96ebc6064e0b.

As we've seen in other Generation We efforts, Zs habitually fight to broadly represent their peers. In climate, that means youth on the front lines or who come from communities that have historically been deprioritized in environmental decisions. They see who has more power and who has less. Greta herself knows that she gets to use her privilege to travel around the world and yell at politicians because she's a White girl from one of the wealthiest countries in northern Europe. A BIPOC girl of the same age living on a frontline island hasn't historically had the same platform.

But youth-led climate organizations intentionally raise up these voices. Nineteen-year-old climate activist Kaylah Brathwaite was born and raised on the island of Saint Croix in the Virgin Islands in the Caribbean. Destructive hurricanes, rising sea levels, and the impact of tourism and oil companies have vastly impacted her island community in a way that is unsustainable for future generations. In an op-ed for *Teen Vogue*, Brathwaite wrote, "I have spent my entire life on a dying planet. We know that climate change not only puts the future of our earth in peril, but it is frontline youth—those of us who live on islands, in rural areas, and along the coast—who will experience its most severe consequences. Climate justice is liberation. And I want to be liberated."

Representation in environmental majors is increasing as well. In past decades, many students who studied environmental studies were perceived as tree huggers or hippies. *White* tree huggers and hippies. Now there's a marked trend for environmental studies majors to be first-generation BIPOC students who have experienced climate change firsthand in their marginalized communities. The result will be a generation of diverse spokespeople able to speak to their own experiences.

That's been accompanied by a rise of youth-led climate groups that focus specifically on underrepresented populations. This includes the International Indigenous Youth Council (IIYC), which represents Indigenous people whose land is often affected by mining, drilling, fracking, and pipelines. This group was instrumental in organizing the Standing Rock protests in an attempt to halt the construction of the Dakota Access Pipeline.

Jasilyn Charger, of the Cheyenne River Sioux tribe, co-founded the IIYC. She used to be a shy teenager but at eighteen became a voice for their entire tribe when they ran 2,000 miles to Washington, DC, to deliver 160,000 signatures to stop the Dakota Access Pipeline. In an interview, they shared their motivation with me: "It's like a calling to my generation. It's been waking up a lot of my people around here. There are so many of our ancestors that fought so hard so we could be here today, and we owe it to them to make sure our seventh generation will still have that same opportunity."

CHANGING LIFESTYLES

Individual lifestyle changes alone won't fix the problem. Zs know that, but it doesn't mean those changes don't make a difference or don't offer Zs some sense of personal control. The scale of the problem is something no one can comprehend, let alone control. But Generation We do take consolation in having control over what they buy or don't buy, eat or don't eat.

Zs believe that we live *with* Earth, not *on* it. Because the health of everything on the planet is interconnected, everything we do impacts the planet and the other people living with it. So that impacts how Generation We shop, what they wear, and what they eat. With that in mind, they're driving four climate-based lifestyle changes: food, fast fashion (as we'll see in the next chapter), transportation, and packaging.

Intersectionality means that even the food Zs put on their plates is a climate-based choice. Generation We grew up watching documentaries on food production and corporate farming that revealed how badly animals are treated and how harmful these practices can be to the planet. Now they are leading a "clean" food revolution, paying much closer attention to where their food is sourced, and the interrelated impact on the health of their bodies and the planet.[85] Around a third of Zs say they have changed their diet due to environmental considerations, and many Zs are exploring vegan or vegetarianism. #Vegan on TikTok now has more than 7 billion views.

As Zs head to college, campuses are having to remake food services. (There was an outcry in the early days of the COVID pandemic in 2020, when New York University students were required to shelter in place and have meat-centric food delivered by the college. One observed on TikTok, "The only thing I could eat was the lettuce from the burger." Zs were appropriately outraged: how can anyone live on lettuce?)

Zs also heavily support local food movements, such as farmers markets and urban or community gardening. They know access to healthy food is unequal, with 19 million people in the United States living in "food deserts," places where at least one-third of the population lacks access to healthy food. Food equality activists addressing the issue include eighteen-year-old high school senior Megan Chen, who founded The Urban Garden Initiative (TUGI), a nonprofit that empowers youth

85   Research by ZSpeak by Global Mosaic, May 2021.

to achieve urban sustainability through a gardening-based educational program. Chen has been able to provide resources and opportunities for lower-income youth to become environmental change makers within their communities. She argues, "A lot of people have the mindset that individual action does nothing. And while one person going low-waste or vegan isn't going to make that much of a difference, community-wide change is how we'll take down these larger systems and make a greater impact."

Pollution from vehicles creates 28 percent of US carbon emissions.[86] Zs point to the photos of smog-free blue skies in Los Angeles during the COVID pandemic as proof of this.

Generation We is turning their backs on cars, at least those with combustion engines. One measure of this is the decrease in the percentage of youth getting drivers' licenses. For teenagers in the past, this was a rite of passage. They counted down the days until they hit sixteen. Zs are much more likely to travel by public transportation, biking, or walking. They look to Europe as a model. In Europe, 49 percent of workers use public transport to get to work versus only 5 percent in the United States.

Zs also have the lowest intention of any generation to buy a car. Of the Zs who already own a car—which is admittedly not yet very many—one-third own an electric vehicle, compared to only 6 percent of boomers.[87] As a twenty-one-year-old in Connecticut said, "Climate change will impact what kind of car I buy. I'm not

86 "Carbon Pollution from Transportation," Environmental Protection Agency, April 1, 2021, https:// www.epa.gov/transportation-air-pollution-and-climate-change/carbon-pollution-transportation.

87 Paul DeCotis and Andrew Dillon, "As Gen Z Leads Electric Vehicle Charge, Costs and Lack of Charging Stations Will Slow Broader Adoption," West Monroe, October 2019, https://www. westmonroe.com/perspectives/point-of-view/as-gen-z-leads-electric-vehicle-charge-costs-and-lack-of-charging-stations-will-slow-broader-adoptio.

going to buy a gas car if it's only going to harm the environment even more." No wonder Tesla became the world's most valuable car company in 2020, and Elon Musk became the world's richest man. That same year, ExxonMobil's share price fell so far that it was kicked off the Dow Jones Industrial Average. The tide seemed to be turning, as incoming President Biden pledged a transition to electric vehicles and even an unreconstructed industrial giant like General Motors said they will eliminate all fossil fuel- burning cars by 2035.

In a high-profile voyage, Greta Thunberg crossed the Atlantic Ocean by boat when she attended the UN climate conference in New York in 2019. It was an inspired decision. Many Zs followed her voyage on social media and, in the process, learned a lot about how much carbon is produced by air travel. (Some critics pointed out that they learned a lot less about the carbon that is also produced by ocean travel, though it is admittedly far lower.)

Now Gen Z can check sites such as shameplane.com to calculate the carbon cost of different lifestyle choices. Flying from London to New York, for example, is directly correlated to the loss of 6.6 square meters of Arctic ice. The website also offers different ways to calculate these personal decisions. For example, how can a traveler offset their flight from Chicago to LA? In this case, options would include going vegan or not driving for the next three months.

Zs' concerns about climate are impacting not only what they buy, but how it's packaged. Older generations felt good once they realized most packaging could be recycled. But Zs can't escape the fact (which they've learned from textbooks, social media, and climate organizations) that only 9 percent of plastic waste is ever actually recycled.[88] So they are upping the ante, seeking products packaged with renewable or compostable plant-based materials, or minimal packaging—and ideally, no packaging at all.

The goal is zero waste, and when Zs find such an item online, it goes viral. And Zs are pretty difficult to stop.

Lush recently created shampoo bars. They look like bars of soap but have zero packaging. Each bar lasts for up to eighty hair washes. In a viral video that generated 75 million views within forty-eight hours and drove 100,000 people to their website, Lush educated the public that 552 million shampoo bottles are disposed of annually. Lush sold out of shampoo bars in forty-eight hours. They now offer package-free mouthwash, in tablet form, with more products forthcoming.

The movement toward package-free products began with a lot of startup companies, but demand has pushed it mainstream. In January 2021, Unilever launched the first-ever deodorant in a refillable stainless steel case from Dove. It comes with an outer package made out of 100 percent Forest Stewardship Council-grade paper, and the customer buys refills and continues to use the same stainless steel deodorant case. Expect to see more of this.

Because Zs are the digital generation, there was a certain inevitability that phone cases would also eventually get the eco treatment. And sure enough, a company called Pela introduced the first compostable phone case, with the goal of "creating a

---

88   Laura Parker, "A Whopping 91 Percent of Plastic Isn't Recycled," National Geographic Society, July 1, 2019, https://www.nationalgeographic.org/article/whopping-91-percent-plastic-isnt-recycled/.

waste-free future." By 2021, they had sold more than 1 million plastic-free phone cases, preventing over 300,000 pounds of plastic waste from entering our ecosystem.

For Zs, moving toward zero waste, minimizing carbon, and having a lower impact on our planet are already a feature of everyday life. To them, the necessity of such actions is a given. Climate is so important that everyone needs to join in—and Zs will call out anyone who doesn't.

THE DECADE TO WATCH

If you go to the Zero Hour website, you'll see a running count-down to the year 2030, down to the second.

Zs know (as does anyone who listens to the science) that this is the critical decade. As Generation We urges us relentlessly, there is no more time to waste. We've made impact with the iceberg and we have to reverse course immediately to avoid a $3\,°C$ or $4\,°C$ future.

Since youth started walking out of schools in 2018 or staged the world's largest climate strike in 2019, momentum has grown. Early in 2021, the United States embraced the most ambitious climate plan in history. In advance of COP 26, the United States hosted a Climate Summit in April 2021 with forty world leaders, where it upped its Paris Agreement commitment, pledging to cut emissions by more than half by 2030 (what the IPCC rec-ommends in order for $1.5\,°C$ to remain feasible). Other countries, including Brazil, Canada, and Japan, immediately followed suit with their own pledges.

We are all interconnected through climate. Carbon emissions

are not a localized issue. A molecule of carbon in the atmosphere circles Earth in less than a week. Every carbon action taken anywhere in the world, positive or negative, affects all of us. What we do in the United States impacts the world immensely, as we are the second largest carbon emitter (after China), but as Generation We knows, the crisis requires global collective action.

As a Gen Xer, I grew up amid the nuclear arms race, with two superpowers—the United States and the Soviet Union—competing to out-innovate each other and build their nuclear arsenal faster than their rivals. Immense investment was driven by the natural ambition of nations to outdo one another.

For the Climate Generation, this decade provides the opportunity for a new, much more productive geopolitical race: a climate race. The victors of the twenty-first century will be the nations that lead the innovation around renewable energy and related technologies such as battery storage. Today's global superpowers—the United States again but also China and the European Union—will be competing on this new frontier.

And as "The Youth of the World" reminded us adults during their Mock COP 26, we can all win through multilateral agreements that leverage the natural ambitions of nations to outdo one another, this time via a race to more and more ambitious emissions targets.

Those are some smart kids.

Z Voices

KAYLAH BRATHWAITE: FRONTLINE ACTIVIST

Twenty-year-old Kaylah Brathwaite (she/her) was born/raised on the frontline island of Saint Croix, US Virgin Islands, has been the director of operations for Zero Hour, is the director of operations for Future Coalition, and is a frontline climate justice activist.

Q: You've spent your life exposed to climate. Tell us about your journey.

A: I was born in Saint Croix in 2001. It's a really, really small island of eighty-four square miles. My dad got a job at the oil refinery. It was one of the largest oil refineries in the West, but they filed for bankruptcy in 2012, and hundreds of folks were laid off, including my dad. Eventually, we moved to North Carolina, which is where I'm at right now. That's where I began to learn about my place in the climate movement. Throughout that, I was just learning a lot about what a just transition could look like. What it would look like if my family didn't have to depend on the very systems that were destroying our homes and our people and the health of the land.

Q: Where did Zero Hour come in?

A: In high school, I wanted to learn more about advocacy and met the former director of operations for Zero Hour. I was interested in Zero Hour because it was one of the only places where I saw Black, non-men having leadership. I had never seen that before. So I was doing work at Zero Hour and I was really getting lost. I was, like, I'm trying to beat the literal clock of climate change, and I burned out. I was depressed for nine months and left to go to a farm in Chapel Hill to get my hands in the dirt and have lovely connections with Black and Indigenous farmers. I learned a lot from them about spirituality and how it can fit into my activism and my practice of taking care of my community. Now that I'm back, one of my passions is backyard gardening, just really loving on the land. It's really restorative for me.

Q: What can we learn from our elders about climate advocacy? Where do you see the roots of their strategies and mobilization in your work now?

A: Our elders and my mentor, Tim Tovan, have taught me a lot about listening to what feels very critical in my soul. Ancestors and elders in the movement like Angela Davis, Assata Shakur, and the women of the Combahee River Collective have given us a lot of language about what justice looks like. Learning from them and having folks share that knowledge with me has been so helpful in directing my energy within the climate justice movement. It's really grounding knowing that we're not just now trying to figure this out. The answers are all there: we just have to listen.

Q: What does climate justice mean to you?

A: It's about protecting and prioritizing the folks that are most in danger from climate change. Materially, it looks like allowing folks who have historically been denied power to redefine what power means.

Q: It feels like we're finally gaining momentum on climate. What gives you hope?

A: I find hope in the people that are working beside me. I find a lot of hope in seeing them exchange wisdom and resources, in seeing them care for one another. So seeing my friends and family doing things that are really incredible or impossible, or even normal, like seeing friends get some sleep because they need to go to sleep or reminding me to get some sleep and take care of myself. Those simple things are great sources of hope.

Q: So many people want to be involved in the climate movement. What advice would you give to them or would you give to your younger self?

A: Something that has been critical to my organizing is taking the time to understand people who are in my bubble or outside it. Watering those relationships and finding love with those people and then taking that love and creating the energy to materially change things around us. The best advice I could give is just to know your neighbors, the people that physically live around you but also the people that share our world. Because understanding how all of our fights for liberation are tied together has been the key to me understanding what it could look like to unravel oppression. People don't put oil refineries near low-income Black communities accidentally. It's all been intentional. Understanding what oppression looks like, understanding where those cracks exist, and filling those cracks by building relationships with people you love is incredibly transformative.

CHAPTER 9

Conscious Capitalism

"Money is power when it comes to making decisions about who and where to buy from. My choosing not to buy from companies that don't share my beliefs is my way of telling companies what's important to me and what changes they should or need to make."

—TWENTY-ONE-YEAR-OLD Z, FLORIDA

For Zs, buying something is not just about making a purchase; it's casting a vote. On how the planet is used. On how workers are treated. On how animals are treated. On who is profiting. On who is marginalized or excluded. On who will have the power.

Each purchase is an investment in the future world Zs are building.

Although Zs know that it's mostly older generations making corporate and governmental decisions right now, they have felt their consumer power. They have seen what they can bolster or boycott when they act collectively. Consumerism is no longer a passive state: it's a form of action.

Of the nearly 8 billion people on the planet, more than 3 billion are Zs.

THE WEALTHIEST GENERATION

Around the world, Generation We make up 40 percent of consumers,[89] with a spending power of over $143 billion.[90] And this is not just their allowances. Only the oldest Zs have formally entered the world of work, but many in this creative generation start earning money at a young age. By middle school, they are hustling, working as creators and influencers, making and selling online, even starting businesses.

As more Zs enter the workforce over the next decade, it's estimated they will surpass the earning power of the millennials. By 2030, Zs will possess 27 percent of the total income in the world.[91] Their financial muscle is going to increase as older generations pass away and wealth is transferred. Grandparents and parents—the Silent Generation and the boomers—will transfer $30 trillion to millennials and Zs in the United States over the next two decades.[92]

That's greater than the wealth of any nation in the world except for the United States and China.

89 Lauryn Chamberlain, "Gen-Z Will Account for 40 Percent of All Consumers by 2020," GeoMarketing by Yext, May 8, 2018.

90 Dominic-Madori Davis, "Gen Zers Have a Spending Power of over $140 Billion, and It's Driving the Frenzy of Retailers and Brands Trying to Win Their Dollars," Business Insider, January 28, 2020.

91 Hillary Hoffower, "Gen Z Is Set to Take Over the Economy in a Decade, despite Potentially Losing $10 Trillion in Earnings because of the Pandemic," Business Insider, November 16, 2020, https://www.businessinsider.com/gen-z-will-take-over-economy-2030-33-trillion-income-2020-11.

92 Mark Hall, "The Greatest Wealth Transfer in History: What's Happening and What Are the Implications?" *Forbes*, November 12, 2019.

What has been called the great wealth transfer has made market-ers—not to mention retailers, manufacturers, banks, investment markets, and any organization that needs to turn a profit—start to pay attention to Zs.

The CEO of Bank of America has predicted that Zs will cause more economic disruption than any previous generation, not just because of their wealth, but because they will bring together their tech savvy with a focus on sustainability and activism.[93] Their money will mostly flow into companies and investments that operate consciously.

THE TRUE VALUE OF THINGS

Much has been written about how Generation We shops online or uses its digital wallet (or even cryptocurrency) rather than credit cards, with predicted consequences ranging from skies dark with delivery drones transporting packages to the death of the penny.

Those things may well happen, but they're not what's important. What's important isn't the process of shopping. It's the decisions Zs take to evaluate purchases and investments.

They look at anything they buy as more than a tangible good or service. Zs' lifelong digital access and awareness of the inter-connectedness of the whole world make them acutely aware of who is making their products, where, in what conditions, how inputs are sourced, the impact on the planet, and more.

---

93 Vicky McKeever, "Gen Z Incomes Predicted to Beat Millennials' in 10 Years and Be 'Most Disruptive Generation Ever,'" CNBC, November 20, 2020, https://www.cnbc.com/2020/11/20/gen-z-incomes-predicted-to-beat-millennials-in-10-years.html.

When I was at school, a rubber plantation was something that existed only in the pages of *Encyclopedia Britannica*. We didn't know where Malaysia is, or how cotton came from Uzbekistan. Generation We can watch people working in those places and find out about their conditions and wages. They know far more about what's going on in the world than we learned from encyclopedias.

Seventy-seven percent of Zs describe themselves as "citizens of the world" (only 20 percent of boomers say the same).[94] If you consider yourself a citizen of the world, it follows that you care about the whole ecosystem.

For Generation We, evaluating purchases in terms of the end-to-end process is just part of living a socially conscious life. They don't see just a supply chain but a whole business ecosystem. And every element within the ecosystem needs to be healthy for it all to work.

As eighteen-year-old environmental entrepreneur Megan Chen explains, "Your money is not simply something you're using just to buy the product. You think about the history of what it took to get your product to your hand: the people who are making it and how it impacts the environment and a lot of other factors. We're living in a world today where it's no longer just about materialistic goods. Companies are the largest contributors to a lot of these environmental issues. We're speaking with our dollars, telling companies, 'This is where I want to spend the money' and I hope that will trickle down. I just hope that it trickles down fast enough."

---

94 Research by ZSpeak by Global Mosaic, May 2021.

Zs know there's often a difference between the price tag and an item's true cost to our planet or to the people or animals that contributed to the making of it. As one twenty-two-year-old in New Jersey said, "We need to shift toward realizing how valuable the environment and sustainability is." That might not prevent Zs from making selfish purchases—indeed, it definitely doesn't—but it does mean that at least they recognize it when they do. They feel guilty about purchases that conflict with their beliefs, which doesn't really help anyone. But they don't make a habit of it, which does.

No Z transaction is just about money. Every dollar is more than just a purchase: it's a statement of their values and beliefs.

To say it again, it's a vote.

EVOLVING CAPITALISM

It mostly comes down to greater *awareness*. That awareness allows Zs to make more conscious choices.

It's an approach dubbed conscious capitalism. It wasn't a Z invention—the term was coined by John Mackey, founder of Whole Foods, (and Raj Sisodia) who famously said, "The conscious capitalism model will show that businesses are the true value creators that can push all of humanity upward for continuous improvement." It matches Zs' beliefs so well that they have effectively co-opted a niche idea into a broad-based movement.

Research suggests that Zs have a less favorable opinion of capitalism than any previous generation. That's only to be expected, given their great access to the full ecosystem it impacts.

Zs see the current version of capitalism as exclusionary and exploitative. It works for some but clearly not for all. They associate the system closely with the boomers, who embraced it as part of their focus on individual advancement (perhaps not intentionally but at the expense of the larger community). In this context, Zs see boomers as a generation of Gordon Gekkos from the movie *Wall Street*—"Greed is good!" While some people benefited from capitalism, many did not.

When Zs see what pollution, the extraction of resources, and rising inequality have done to the planet—and they can't escape it because it's on TikTok and other social media platforms all the time—they look around to see who's pocketed all the money. Guess what? The boomers control 70 percent of all disposable income in the United States.[95] It doesn't take Sherlock Holmes to figure out who got the cash from the great capitalism heist.

Just as Zs are changing other systems to be more inclusive, representative, and mindful of intersectional impacts, so they're challenging capitalism to do the same. As a seventeen-year-old from Ohio said, "I would like to see capitalism start to serve people and the planet for the first time. Capitalism throughout history has mostly served companies and the rich, not everyday people."

Studies have also suggested that Zs have a more favorable opinion of socialism—and that's the kind of assertion that sends shockwaves through a political establishment in which socialism has been a dirty word for decades.

From our research, I don't take it to mean Zs are really socialist, or at least not in the traditional economic sense of running a

95 "Baby Boomer Report," US News Market Insights, 2015, https://www.usnews.com/pubfiles/
    USNews_Market_Insights_Boomers2015.pdf.

planned economy. They use it more as a shorthand for wanting a more socially conscious type of capitalism that is more inclusive. In my conversations with Zs, many refer to Bernie Sanders's popularization of the term "democratic socialist," which appealed to them because it was connected with policies such as universal healthcare and free college education. As a twenty-one-year-old in Florida explained, "I think that capitalism is the root of many societal issues today. In order for people to be better served, things like healthcare need to be taken out of private ownership and need to be granted as inalienable rights by the government. Capitalism isn't serving people if some are starving to death and living on the streets while others won't share the resources because it won't make them money."

WE, NOT ME

Zs don't have to look far for evidence that the boomers' credo "Hard work always pays" doesn't apply today. The generation immediately above them, the millennials, are well known to be worse off economically than their parents. And not just a little worse off. Many millennials are burdened with huge debt from skyrocketing college costs that they can't pay back because of economic crises and a changing job market. They're more likely to live at home than other generations and less likely to own a home (the highest rate of home ownership is—surprise, surprise—among boomers). When Generation X were in their early thirties, they owned 8 percent of the nation's wealth; at the same age, millennials own just 3 percent of national wealth. The boomers are worth a whopping twenty times more than the millennials.[96]

---

96   Christopher Ingraham, "The Staggering Millennial Wealth Deficit, in One Chart," *The Washington Post*, December 3, 2019, https://www.washingtonpost.com/business/2019/12/03/precariousness-modern-young-adulthood-one-chart/.

For Zs and millennials, stories about the golden years of prosperity after World War II ring hollow. In their eyes, it feels as if they function in a system in which their elders have kept everything for themselves, while willfully ignoring the opportunity to invest in education or social programs that might have benefited Americans for generations into the twenty-first century. In other words, it feels like greed.

Their elders selfishly hoarded resources and spiked inequality to previously unimaginable highs. And the younger generations got screwed.

It's not just about being screwed, though. It's also about feeling sick. Me-based capitalism is antithetical to Zs' we-based values.

Plus, it clearly doesn't work. The idea that millennials and Zs could put their heads down, study and work hard, and then inherit the kind of job security and comfortable homes and lifestyles their parents enjoyed is nothing but a mirage, a figment of boomer imaginations that were addled by living through a bubble that has long burst. This is the trajectory Zs were raised to expect but now see through. It became clear this wasn't in the cards for them much earlier on in their lives than it did for the millennials.

The United States, the world's largest economy, has the second-highest rate of poverty among the countries of the developed world. Almost one in ten Americans live in poverty,[97] and 35

---

97 Linda Giannarelli, Laura Wheaton, and Gregory Acs, "2020 Poverty Projections," Urban Institute, July 2020, https://www.urban.org/sites/default/files/publication/102521/2020-poverty-projections.pdf.

percent of children suffer from food insecurity,[98] which means they frequently go to bed hungry.

Income inequality is only increasing. Inflation-adjusted middle-class wages have essentially been frozen for forty years, while the earnings of the top 1 percent have tripled.[99] While 40 million Americans filed for unemployment[100] and the country was in the midst of an eviction crisis during the COVID pandemic in 2020, tax breaks and other changes meant that billionaires saw their net worth increase by half a trillion dollars.[101]

Zs take all of this in online. And because they're online, the information they're absorbing is unmoderated. There are no economists or academic experts explaining why things must be the way they are, no modifying voices to justify inequity or "trickle-down" economic strategies. Without those voices to stand up for the system, the system is exposed for what it is: massively inequitable to huge portions of the population, including youth.

Like the emperor's new clothes, the system depends on enough people believing the illusion.

Zs sometimes call traditional capitalism *extractive capitalism*.

---

98 Lauren Bauer, "The COVID-19 Crisis Has Already Left Too Many Children Hungry in America," Brookings, May 6, 2020, https://www.brookings.edu/blog/up-front/2020/05/06/the-COVID-19-crisis-has-already-left-too-many-children-hungry-in-america/.

99 Drew DeSilver, "For Most Americans, Real Wages Have Barely Budged for Decades," Pew Research Center, May 30, 2020, https://www.pewresearch.org/fact-tank/2018/08/07/for-most-us-workers-real-wages-have-barely-budged-for-decades/.

100 "U.S. Jobless Claims Pass 40 Million: Live Business Updates," *The New York Times*, May 28, 2020, https://www.nytimes.com/2020/05/28/business/unemployment-stock-market-coronavirus.html.

101 Hiatt Woods, "How Billionaires Saw Their Net Worth Increase by Half a Trillion Dollars during the Pandemic," Business Insider, October 30, 2020, https://www.businessinsider.com/billionaires-net-worth-increases-coronavirus-pandemic-2020-7.

It extracts wealth from the earth, from workers, and from communities. It has polluted the air, degraded the water and soil, and destroyed biodiversity.

In contrast, Zs advocate for a form of capitalism where corporations have a purpose beyond just achieving profits. This is sometimes referred to as the triple bottom line: serving profit, people, and the planet. The idea is to serve the interests of *all* stakeholders in the whole ecosystem, not just the executives and shareholders. This is critical because a lot of the stakeholders in the ecosystem can't speak for themselves. The marginalized populations who grow food or make sneakers, the animals that produce milk, the oceans that give us fish, or the forests that give us their trees don't have a voice.

LEGAL CHANGES

Conscious capitalism is already being translated into a legal framework for economic activity. Based on the model of the C Corp, which is a regular corporation, a new business entity has appeared: the B Corp, or "benefit corporation." A B Corp is a for-profit, like a C Corp, but with far more stringent standards for social and environmental performance. B Corps have to be completely transparent and publish all details about their operations, and every year they're reviewed and graded by a nonprofit named B Lab to grade how they're doing.

A B Corp signs on for a lot more work and scrutiny than a regular corporation, so it's not to be taken on lightly, but it is a prized designation that more and more businesses conclude will be worth the effort in a marketplace with growing numbers of millennials and Zs. There were more than 3,000

B Corps at the start of 2021,[102] and the number is growing exponentially thanks to customer demand. These companies include Patagonia, one of the first B Corps and a flag bearer of the movement, and Athleta, which transitioned from C Corp to B Corp in 2018[103] and experienced spikes not just in sales but also in the number of Gen Zs who wanted to work there. In the future, recruiting the top people may become more difficult without B Corp status.

Generation We is also starting its own companies to work in more ethical ways. Estella Struck was a college sophomore with time on her hands during COVID who parlayed her passion for thrifting into an online clothing company that sells second-hand clothing in auctions she drops on Instagram and TikTok. Emma Chamberlain became a YouTube influencer when she was sixteen and at nineteen created an eco-friendly company to address the ills of the coffee industry. She uses sustainably sourced organic coffee to make low-waste coffee bags, similar to tea bags, and she pays her suppliers fair prices to provide economic stability for the coffee farmers.[104]

AT THE STORE

Zs expect companies to provide end-to-end transparency, so they use conscious capitalism apps, such as DollarSpeak or Buycott, to check their purchases. Another app, GoodGuide, lists more than 150,000 products according to how safe they

---

102 "A Global Community of Leaders," Certified B Corporation, 2021, https://bcorporation.net.

103 Christopher Marquis, "Athleta Builds B Corp Awareness while Finding Strength in Community," Medium. B The Change, August 12, 2020, https://bthechange.com/athleta-builds-b-corp-awareness-while-finding-strength-in-community-138fb136b483.

104 "Our Coffee: It's More than a Drink," Chamberlain Coffee, 2021, https://chamberlaincoffee.com/pages/our-coffee.

are to use, how healthy they are, how green they are, and how socially responsible they are. The consumer holds the app up to the barcode, and the app rates the producer's record on the environment, social issues, and transparency.

Zs also expect companies to pivot to address issues as they arise. Operating consciously doesn't just mean being conscious of what's going on; it means reacting to it and taking a leadership stance. When the Trump administration introduced immigration bans in 2017, for example, Airbnb responded by providing free short-term housing to 100,000 refugees. Zs were watching to see which companies were meaningfully supporting racial justice in the summer of 2020: "Nike stood up for the Black community during the marches in summer 2020, and in doing so showed immense support but also was the first step in getting other companies to show where they stand," said a twenty-one-year-old from Missouri. As evidence that companies are increasingly embracing their values, many responded swiftly to Georgia's passing of a law to limit voter access in spring 2021. A seventeen-year-old in Ohio told us, "Oh yes, I admired the MLB for taking the all-star game out of Atlanta because it shows that even businesses will take themselves to a place where they haven't passed a discriminatory law."

As conscious consumers, this stuff really matters to Zs. As teenagers, of course, they will sometimes buy what they want or are craving in the moment, but on balance, a larger percentage of their dollars will increasingly go to the companies with which they align. This twenty-two-year-old in New Mexico describes how she feels about Starbucks: "I absolutely think companies should take a stand on social issues. Is Starbucks the best place to get coffee from? Not necessarily, but because they have shown support for Black Lives Matter and Pride and donate a portion of their proceeds to Planned Parenthood, I'm going to continue to spend my money there."

Generation We is savvy enough to know when a company is taking meaningful action rather than simply jumping on a band-wagon, as a twenty-year-old in Florida explained: "I admire companies that speak on relevant issues, like when fashion brands speak out against fast fashion and unethically sourced labor, but when companies like Walmart make a statement on something like police brutality, it feels very much like they are pandering without doing anything to enact real change. Walmart is a billion-dollar corporation that could single-handedly solve some of our crises."

FAST FASHION

Zs habitually research a purchase online before they make it, not just to check the supplier credentials but also to get a bargain. They are savvy value seekers who don't want to pay more than they have to, but that can lead them into a moral minefield.

The problem is most acute in fashion and particularly in fast fashion (stores or brands whose stock rotates rapidly, sometimes once a week or even quicker). A twenty-three-year-old from Illinois found a dress she liked online and discovered that it was offered by multiple companies. She researched it and learned it was made in Malaysia, in a factory that probably wasn't great for its workers. That's how endemic exploitation is in the industry.

Ultimately, she ended up buying the dress because she liked it and couldn't afford something more expensive that was more sustainable. Which just goes to show that Zs are far from perfect or immune to external pressure. Let's face it: sometimes they can't resist a bargain. They're no less vain or able to resist peer pressure to look good than other young people (and most are still pretty broke). But they do see a cute shirt as more than just a cute shirt—it becomes either a statement of their values and beliefs or the cause of an embarrassed apology. Zs will actually say to one another, "I'm so embarrassed I bought this from Shein...I know I shouldn't have, but it was so cute. I'll thrift it when I'm finished with it, though, so that will help."

This makes Zs highly conflicted because they go into the capitalist system with eyes wide open.

Zs are leading a retail revolution toward what they term sustainable fashion. They're buying less but trading, thrifting, and renting more. Lauren Singer, the first eco-influencer to achieve real fame—there are a small army of them online now—terms herself "a zero-waste environmentalist trying to make the world less trashy." Her blog, *Trash Is for Tossers*, is an account of living a zero-waste lifestyle, or at least a very low-waste one, that encourages Zs to do the same, because she makes it sound both noble and fun. She also came up with packagefreeshop.com, a website where Zs can search for more sustainable product alternatives.

Fast fashion is Zs' single largest expenditure, and it accounts for 10 percent of the world's annual total emissions,[105] so it's a huge part of their conscious capitalism approach. As the most photographed generation, Zs are constantly taking pictures of themselves and each other. That means they want to look good.

---

105 "Clothes and Climate Change: How a Fashion Choice Change Could Lead to Better Air Quality: Group against Smog and Pollution," Pgh.org. July 28, 2020, https://gasp-pgh.org/2020/07/28/clothes-climate-change-how-a-fashion-choice-change-could-lead-to-better-air-quality/.

They buy fashion with a different mindset (and not just because they buy online without trying things on). They are the first generation to have to balance wanting to look good with the full knowledge that the fashion industry is one of the worst offenders of environmental degradation, of worker exploitation, and of pollution. The average pair of jeans produces seventy-four pounds of CO_2. A single new T-shirt requires about 700 gallons of water, and the UN says the fashion industry produces 20 percent of global wastewater.[106] The Environmental Protection Agency estimates that 26 billion pounds of textiles end up in landfill every year.

In a way, that's the whole point about fast fashion. Consumers don't buy it because they need it. They just want it. It's a cheap and disposable form of almost instant self-gratification. You wear it, you toss it, and you buy something new.

Zs are leading a backlash against fast fashion because it embodies all the worst corporate behavior. The irony is that fast fashion is targeted mostly at Zs. Companies like Amazon have a huge presence on TikTok and Instagram to reach out to Zs who they know love to express themselves by buying clothes, but who also have limited funds.

There's a clear contradiction between Zs' protests against fast fashion and the fact that they continue to buy it. During the first three months of the pandemic in 2020, the sales of the most popular fast fashion firm Boohoo rose 45 percent.[107] Zs were

---

106 "How Much Do Our Wardrobes Cost to the Environment?" World Bank, September 23, 2019, https://www.worldbank.org/en/news/feature/2019/09/23/costo-moda-medio-ambiente.

107 Caroline Leaper, "Boohoo's 45 Per Cent Rise in Sales Shows That Scandal Won't Stop Fast Fashion Shoppers," *The Telegraph*, September 30, 2020, https://www.telegraph.co.uk/fashion/brands/boohoos-45-per-cent-rise-sales-shows-scandal-wont-stop-fast/.

at home and bored, so they cheered themselves up by buying clothes.

At least they had the decency to feel bad about buying them. Or they consoled themselves with the thought that when they had finished with a garment, they would thrift it.

#THRIFTHAUL

As part of the new approach to fashion, thrifting has become cool (it's also become a verb, *to thrift*). It's no longer connotated with being destitute and sifting through piles of damp, off-smelling knitwear. Trading online has made thrifting far cooler, and the increased time indoors during the pandemic sent Zs to their closets to start selling clothes they didn't want. They set up their own stores online and modeled their old or curated clothes to sell. The people who snap the clothes up display their bargains with the hashtag #ThriftHaul on TikTok; it currently has 430 million views.

The thrifting and secondhand markets are a sustainable alternative to fast fashion, and they come at little or no cost to the individual or the environment. They turn fashion into something circular, where a particular user becomes just a part of a garment's life cycle because it's been used before and it will be reused again. It turns even fast fashion into a more sustainable option because it reduces new purchases, keeping pieces in circulation and out of landfills.

Circular fashion got an endorsement from an unlikely source when Anna Wintour, editor of *Vogue* and high priestess of traditional fashion, recently promoted it as a way of valuing the clothes you own: wearing them again and again, then passing them on.

Of course, when it comes to fashion, if *Vogue* is onboard, you're on trend. Meghan Markle modeled this when she was intentionally photographed wearing the same outfits multiple times; Oxfam began the #SecondhandSeptember campaign, challenging celebrities to go a month without buying or wearing anything new; and even the country's most overtly fashion-conscious family launched a resale apparel site, Kardashian Kloset.

For Zs, thrift and reuse have an additional benefit. They fit perfectly with Zs' dislike of ticking boxes and their desire to be and look unique. Buy new, and you'll likely be wearing the same Urban Outfitter shirt as everybody else. Buy secondhand, you'll be one of a kind.

Secondhand (or perhaps "pre-loved") clothes are predicted to more than double into a $64 billion market by 2025. While retail generally shrank by 15 percent during COVID in 2020, the online secondhand market grew 69 percent, and 40 percent of Zs said they had bought secondhand apparel, footwear, or accessories.[108]

Many Z transactions don't involve retailers; they're completed on apps like Depop that let Zs buy and sell clothes peer-to-peer. A popular model is to create your own online shop with a distinct style, then curate specific secondhand pieces (sourced from other online or IRL thrift outlets) and then "drop" these new collections to followers. When the pandemic began, Depop saw a 90 percent increase in traffic, which they used to raise $62

---

108 "2020 Fashion Resale Market and Trend Report," thredUP, 2020, https://www.thredup.com/resale/.

million in funding. As many as 90 percent of their active users are under the age of twenty-four.[109]

Another app, TradeMade, doesn't involve money or even exchange. It's based on the idea that the world has enough underused or unwanted clothing floating around to get everyone what they want. Things just need to find the right home. A similar site, thredUP, has recirculated 4 million fast fashion items, which they calculate has saved about 5.5 million pounds of textile waste.[110]

Generation We love that sort of math. They're used to handling data, so reuse and recycling sites keep them informed about exactly how much waste they're avoiding or how much carbon they're saving. The act of buying is pretty intangible—tapping a screen—but the numbers prove what a difference they're making. They see it right in front of them.

And that makes it cool, which is key: no fashion survives being uncool. As many as 80 percent of Zs said there was no stigma to buying secondhand; more than half said they actually felt proud to buy secondhand—and guilty when they buy fast fashion.[111]

Mainstream retailers are already losing dollars to the secondhand and thrifting industry, so they want to get on board. Gen Z brands like Abercrombie & Fitch, Hollister, and Reebok are now partnering with resale sites such as thredUP and eBay, where

---

109 Mary Hanbury, "A Social Shopping App That's like a Mix of eBay and Instagram Just Raised $62 Million to Triple Its US Users," Business Insider, June 7, 2019, https://www.businessinsider.com/shopping-app-depop-raises-62-million-and-plans-us-expansion-2019-6.

110 "2020 Fashion Resale Market and Trend Report," thredUP, 2020, https://www.thredup.com/resale/.

111 Ibid.

customers can buy used Abercrombie & Fitch from...Abercrombie & Fitch.

Another trend Zs are jumping onboard with is renting. They pay a monthly membership to rent lightly used clothes. With Express's Express Style Trial, for example, users can rent unlimited clothes every month with free shipping and exchanges. American Eagle does the same. And if you decide you want to purchase something, you get it at a discount.

The Guardian in the UK predicts that if everyone adopts Gen Z habits, there will be a shift to a new normal where consumer wardrobes feature a range of resale and rented items alongside new.[112]

THE GREAT WEALTH TRANSFER

The whole financial industry is preparing for the great wealth transfer.

Where investment money flows when that $30 trillion changes hands will be shaped by what Zs and millennials value versus what the boomers and silents valued.

The industry is banking on the rise of ESG (environmental, social, and governance) investing. ESG investing is about achieving positive financial returns while also having a positive impact on the environment and society.

Financial institutions in tune with Generation We see the

---

112 Priya Elan, "Shopping Habits of Generation Z Could Spell the End of Fast Fashion," *The Guardian*, May 25, 2020, https://www.theguardian.com/fashion/2020/may/25/shopping-habits-of-generation-z-could-spell-end-of-fast-fashion.

coming transition to a net-zero carbon economy as the greatest commercial opportunity of our time for the financial sector because of the rise of new investment categories. There's renewable energy, like wind or solar, but there's also natural capital, which means investing in nature: regenerative agriculture, reforestation, water management, and so on.

The World Economic Forum predicts that investing in nature (such as reforestation of coastal wetlands or sustainable management of farmlands) will create $10 trillion of economic growth and 395 million jobs by 2030.[113]

Sustainability is no longer niche. It's no longer a luxury consideration. It's at the top of the balance sheet. COVID elevated everyone's awareness of the interconnectedness of things, which increased the demand for sustainable investing. In the words of Citibank executive Philip Drury, "COVID has taken the ESG debate to a whole other level. COVID is not a financial crisis. It's a global health pandemic that touches everybody. And the environment affects everybody. The current crisis has created a new sense of urgency." The *Financial Times* argued that offering ESG investments had become a competitive necessity for financial firms.

Not many Zs are investing yet, although some have jobs or a 401(k), but a Bank of America study found that 80 percent say they factor ESG into their investing decisions.[114]

---

113 Amanda Russo and Max Hall, "395 Million New Jobs by 2030 if Businesses Prioritize Nature, Says World Economic Forum," World Economic Forum, July 14, 2020, https://www.weforum.org/press/2020/07/395-million-new-jobs-by-2030-if-businesses-prioritize-nature-says-world-economic-forum/.

114 "Thematic Investing OK Zoomer: Gen Z Primer," Bank of America Merrill Lynch, December 1, 2020, https://www.bofaml.com/content/dam/boamlimages/documents/articles/ID21_0026/GenZ_redacted.pdf.

When Barclays surveyed its high-net-worth customers (mostly boomers and above), they found that 68 percent were already being pushed toward more sustainable investing in their family investments by their children and grandchildren.[115] So even Zs who aren't yet investing for themselves are influencing investment decisions.

Generation We has figured out that just as business has contributed to our problems, it can be flipped to be a big part of the solution. The fossil fuel crisis is highly unlikely to be solved by a bunch of kids in the streets, simply waving banners. The collective power of over 3 billion global Zs with $143 billion in spending power and up to $30 trillion in wealth transfer for US Zs to invest is going to force a revolution in corporate and financial institution priorities.

Trust me. You will want to be on the right side of this when it happens.

---

115 Bérengère Sim, "Here's How Gen Z is Pushing Wealthy Parents to Remake Their Investment Portfolios, Says Barclays," Financial News, November 23, 2020, https://www.fnlondon.com/articles/wealthy-investors-pushed-to-green-investments-by-children-and-grandchildren-says-barclays-20201123.

Z Voices

ESTELLA STRUCK: THE DISRUPTOR

Twenty-year-old Estella Struck (she/her) is an environmental entrepreneur who used her year of "remote learning" to create one of the fastest-growing Gen Z secondhand fashion brands to counter fast fashion.

Q: Can you tell us about your story and how you got into sustainability?

A: During quarantine in 2020, I had so much free time once my freshman year ended. And I have always been interested in climate change and solutions because obviously I do have climate anxiety and it's going to affect us all. So I really dove into learning about the fashion industry and I was like, oh okay, I've been thrifting for a really long time, but I didn't really think about how it was helping our planet because I had never been taught that. When I was in college, I saw my peers always buy so many new clothes, and I had never really thought about buying so many clothes for no reason. I thought, here's a simple little solution and dropped twenty secondhand items online. Then I went really, really viral.

Q: What would you like to build to?

A: I think that this could be the secondhand clothing store brand for Gen Z. A lot of fast fashion brands are multibillion-dollar corporations that are huge and pervasive. But I am giving people who can shop at a Princess Polly a sustainable option that is kind of the same style. I really want to give people who rely on fast fashion, who aren't really thinking about being eco-friendly, a way to purchase sustainably. They're voting with their dollar without really realizing it, but also, when they follow me, they're learning about this stuff inadvertently.

It's crazy because when we think of sustainability, we think of buying all these really expensive products and living zero waste. But you don't have to do that. It looks different for everyone and it's super important to figure out what sustainability looks like for you. I like using my platform to show people what it looks like for me as a regular everyday person, because I don't consider myself really to be an environmentalist. I care about the planet, but I do feel that word is a little loaded. I just want to show people that it's easy to care about the planet and think about your own impact.

Q: Can you talk more about imperfect environmentalism?

A: It's not going to be the people who are being perfect and are shopping secondhand and being vegan and avoiding plastic who are going to save our planet. It's all of us doing one of those things kind of well, it's all of us. It's almost 8 billion of us. If everyone in the United States bought one secondhand item instead of new per year, that's 5.7 billion pounds of carbon saved per year. So that one little tiny switch has a huge impact if we do it collectively. So that's my message: you don't have to take on all the responsibility; it's just collective action.

Q: Has this affected your own eco-anxiety?

A: It has. I want my community to feel empowered in their ability to make change because I feel like everyone thinks, "Oh, I'm just one person," but we're all one person and we can all do something. And if we're all doing it together, then it's really going to have a big impact on the planet and the future. And it's scary to think about. I have climate anxiety a lot. But when I just think I'm doing something, these people are doing something and they're starting these conversations, and I can see when I share fact posts how many people put it on their stories and they're educating their friends. It's like a spider web, and it just makes me feel a lot better about where we are.

Q: What are some of your ideas about how capitalism can better serve us and the planet?

A: I didn't realize how much money there was in the world until I went to college. I went to a school that was only 30 percent on financial aid and stuff. So there's a lot of money in the world and we have the ability to do good. I'm trying to use fashion as a force for good. We can use capitalism as a force for good. It's just about a revolution of consciousness, I feel, because we're born into a society that has these binaries and you have to be taught or educated or exposed to a different way of thinking. I feel like it's going to take a lot of work to get people to use capitalism for good and realize that you really can make change through voting with your dollar and spending your money and investing in what you believe in.

Generation We the People

"During the 2016 election, I was sixteen and everybody around me had opinions that were so polarizing and I was in the middle of all of it. It was hard not to become engaged because it seemed like the stakes were so high. Even though I couldn't vote yet, I quickly developed my own opinions and beliefs. I will be able to vote in the upcoming election and it is super important to me."

—TWENTY-YEAR-OLD Z, OKLAHOMA

If Zs and millennials hadn't turned out in such high numbers, Donald Trump would have won the 2020 presidential election. They drove Joe Biden's margins up more than any other age cohort. If the election had been based only on voters over forty-five years of age, Trump would have been reelected.[116]

Bear in mind that in 2020, only a third of Generation We were old enough to vote. Their political power is only going to increase

---

116 "Election Week 2020: Young People Increase Turnout, Lead Biden to Victory," CIRCLE at Tufts, November 25, 2020, https://circle.tufts.edu/latest-research/election-week-2020.

GENERATION WE THE PEOPLE · 213

as more of them come of age. That will have profound ramifications for the system, for both main parties and for everyone.

(A note of clarification: most election data are recorded for ages eighteen to twenty-nine, which effectively combines Zs and the youngest third of millennials together.)

There's a track record of the youth bloc not showing up for elections. In the 2016 presidential election, only 42–44 percent of youth voted, allowing for margin of error. But in 2020, 52–55 percent of youth voted.[117] Youth made up 17 percent of all votes cast.

To put it another way, nearly one in five voters was in their teens or twenties.

This election represented the first chance Zs had to show up (in 2016, the oldest Zs were nineteen, so only a small slice could vote), and they took it. No wonder. Generation We was desperate for the chance to have a say. For the previous four years, they had experienced the antagonism of a president whose personal views and politics went against their collective ethos and ran counter to their priority issues. They'd watched US politics became so polarized that the process would ultimately lead to citizens storming Capitol Hill to protest the results of an election all neutral observers and the courts of law said was entirely fair.

It's probably no surprise that when Zs finally got the chance to weigh in, they took it.

It's been a commonplace belief among young people in the

---

117 Ibid.

past that there's not much to choose between parties at election time. This belief probably reflects the typical difficulty the young have in seeing how politics relates to their lives—which are, in any case, full of many other distractions. Why show up only to choose between two old White guys who won't really impact your life?

In 2020, Zs could see a clear choice. They happened to reach political maturity during one of the most divisive administrations in history and perhaps the most divisive political era since the Civil War. Whereas earlier generations recall periods of more or less bipartisan cooperation, for someone aged eighteen, the first political debate they might have seen in their lives was the train wreck between Trump and Biden in September 2020. The oldest Zs might remember when Trump infamously stalked Hillary Clinton on stage during a 2016 debate, which immediately became a meme and an SNL skit set to music from the movie *Jaws*. Zs can't believe that level of divisiveness. They can see that such division is unsustainable.

Perhaps for the rest of us, this realization has dawned more gradually; like the frog in the boiling pot, we don't perceive the severity of the situation until it's too late. Generation We recognize that the country's (and the world's) problems require bipartisan cooperation to solve. And they've never seen anything like that.

In this way, the members of Congress who backed Trump's allegations of a stolen election were shortsighted. They were not thinking about their own future careers. Young people were watching and shaking their heads as they watched one Republican politician after another prioritize their own political ambitions over the integrity of the democratic system. Nearly nine in ten Zs said Biden's election was legitimate, and the same number described the resulting storming of the Capitol on January 6, 2021, as "anti-American."[118] The participants and the defenders of their actions only further alienated Zs.

THREE TYPES OF CHANGE

Three fundamental areas of politics will change under pressure from Zs—and in largely predictable ways: voter demographics, political priorities, and the political system and how it works. In other words, virtually everything.

DEMOGRAPHICS

Zs represent 27 percent of the US population.[119] In the 2016 presidential election, only Zs born in 1997 and 1998 could vote. In 2020, the first five-and-a-half years' worth of Zs could vote, making up 10 percent of eligible voters. These numbers will be larger by 2024, and by 2028, all but the very youngest Zs will be able to vote.

For a long time, politics has been a boomer playground. In the 2000 election, when Al Gore won the popular vote but a Supreme Court ruling gave the White House to George W. Bush—remember the hanging chads in Miami-Dade County?—the election came down to 537 votes in Florida.[120] In that election, boomers and older made up 68 percent of the electorate.[121]

118 Research by ZSpeak by Global Mosaic, May 2021.

119 "Generation Z: Latest Gen Z News, Research, Facts and Strategies," Business Insider, 2021, https://www.businessinsider.com/generation-z.

120 "Bush Is Declared Winner in Florida, but Gore Vows to Contest Results," *The New York Times*, November 26, 2000, https://www.nytimes.com/2000/11/26/politics/bush-is-declared-winner-in-florida-but-gore-vows-to-contest-results.html.

121 "Voting and Registration in the Election of November 2000," US Census Bureau, February 2002, https://www.census.gov/data/tables/2000/demo/voting-and-registration/p20-542.html.

For twenty years, our politics, priorities, and electoral results have been a boomer show.

In the 2020 election, Gen Z and millennials combined matched the boomers—about 40 percent each—and their views, which lean liberal, canceled out the boomers' conservative tilt.

The math is only going to get worse for conservatives as more Zs enter the electorate.

Demographics alone suggest it's possible there won't be another Republican president in our lifetime (though other factors could make it possible, as we'll see).

Of course, youth of all generations tend to be more idealistic and liberal than their elders before they start paying taxes, owning properties, and raising families. The difference this time is that a combination of the demographics and the political moment might mean that Zs start left and stay left.

In *The Kids Are All Left: How Young Voters Will Unite America*, political scientist David Faris[122] predicts that Zs, united by their progressive values and ideas, will end the deep divisions in US politics and shatter the partisan stalemate. Although Zs represent a range of ideology, their overwhelming progressive stance on key issues like climate suggest the Republican Party will have to shift its position to retain any relevancy.

The move away from boomer-dominated politics will be a pivot point.

---

122 Hoboken, NJ: Melville House Publishing, 2020.

We've seen that Generation We will be the first non-White majority generation. For the first time, what were historically minority issues are now majority issues. For the first time in the 2020 election, one-third of voters were BIPOC. In nine of the swing states, including Arizona and Georgia, BIPOC youth tipped the vote toward a victory for Biden. He won Arizona by only 10,000 votes, and it was the eighteen- to twenty-nine-year-olds who gave him the largest margin over Trump: 24 percent, or about 315,000 votes. In Georgia, eighteen- to twenty-nine-year-olds made up 21 percent of all votes cast, and they favored Biden by eighteen points. Ninety percent of Black youth voted for Biden, compared to only 8 percent for Trump.[123]

BIPOC youth reported three issues that sent them to the polls in such huge numbers: racial equity, police violence, and the disproportionate impact of COVID on their communities. The first two will remain political priorities, whether politicians want them to be or not. Altering the current of demographics is as fruitless as trying to halt time.

More than half of boomers were born before Rosa Parks refused to give up her seat on the bus in 1955, igniting the civil rights movement. That's right: over half of boomers predate the modern civil rights movement. Now BIPOC are determining election results on a national scale, even as they are subjected to growing voter suppression efforts to counter their power.

POLITICAL PRIORITIES

Generation We are lifelong civic actors. Long before they could vote, they walked out of school to support gun regulation, cli-

---

123 Angela Nelson, "Young Voters Were Crucial to Biden's Win," *Tufts Now*, November 12, 2020, https://now.tufts.edu/articles/young-voters-were-crucial-to-biden-s-win.

mate action, or racial justice. Many were only in elementary school when they took to the street for the first time or started pushing political ideas out on social media.

It's no wonder they showed up at the polls in such high numbers.

Because they've been involved, they understand how hard it is to change public policy. They're realists, not idealists. They understand that taking to the streets or posting their views on social media isn't enough to get results. They need to vote, too. They need to do it *all*.

Thanks to their social media and activism, Generation We is immersed in politics. They dismiss older generations who just show up and vote every two to four years, because years of history classes have taught Zs that issues don't run in four-year cycles. They understand that democracy is a verb, not a static state. As one said, "I've learned that you need to be constantly working to maintain what's working and to move the system forward." More than three-quarters of young voters said they believe they have the power and responsibility to change the country and that this work goes beyond elections.[124]

Historically, the youth cohort always has the lowest turnout rate in an election. When Donald Trump was elected in 2016, only 42–44 percent of youth aged eighteen to twenty-nine showed up. They voted overwhelmingly for Hillary Clinton, and if more had shown up, she would have won.

After watching Trump's White House gut their priority issues,

---

124 Kristian Lundberg, Abby Kiesa, and Alberto Medina, "The 2020 Election Is Over, but Young People Believe in Continued Engagement," CIRCLE at Tufts, January 12, 2021, https://circle.tufts.edu/latest-research/2020-election-over-young-people-believe-continued-engagement.

youth repented when the midterms came in 2018. Boy, did they show up that time; there was a seventeen-point bump in the youth vote, and it wasn't even a presidential election.[125] The Marjory Stoneman Douglas school shooting in Florida earlier that year had also stoked Generation We's political involvement.

Prior to the 2020 election, we asked Zs if they thought the country was headed in the right direction: only 11 percent said yes. Even less—8 percent—thought the government understood Gen Z's priority issues.[126]

So they rallied. Big time. And they hedged their bets. These digital natives fired it up in advance of the election, with 45 percent actually creating content—such as a video, GIF, or image—to raise awareness about a political issue on YouTube, Instagram, TikTok, or Snapchat. And BIPOC youth were even more civically active, with 56 percent of Black and 57 percent of Latinx youth putting their personal experiences into the world to raise awareness.[127]

Boomers have driven a "hands-off" approach to many issues, but Generation We believes more than any other generation in solving social problems through government involvement. The idea of small government has been a fixture of US politics for the last several decades, but it's now under threat. Zs clearly see that issues like climate change aren't going to be solved without systemic overhaul and government leadership. Left entirely to

125 "Election Night 2018: Historically High Youth Turnout, Support for Democrats," CIRCLE at Tufts, November 7, 2018, https://circle.tufts.edu/latest-research/election-night-2018-historically-high-youth-turnout-support-democrats.

126 Research by ZSpeak by Global Mosaic, November 2020.

127 Ruby Belle Booth et al., "Young People Turn to Online Political Engagement during COVID-19," CIRCLE at Tufts, October 20, 2020, https://circle.tufts.edu/latest-research/young-people-turn-online-political-engagement-during-COVID-19.

itself, the economic system isn't going to create more equity or protect the planet. When asked if the government should be doing more to solve problems, only 23 percent of boomers and 38 percent of millennials agreed—but a whopping (and majority) 52 percent of Gen Z agreed.[128]

That's another boomer article of faith gone.

Zs are frustrated by a democracy that doesn't seem to represent the will of its people. An eighteen-year-old from Ohio ranted, "The government hasn't done anything about the police system we've been protesting about for months." And a twenty-two-year-old from Delaware insisted, "Democracy means each person's voice is heard and counted. This is being taken from many people if the US continues to make it difficult to vote for certain demographics."

To put it lightly, there's huge latent demand for change.

POLITICAL SYSTEM

Generation We doesn't only want to change the issues on the table; they also want to change the rules of the game. Specifically, they believe the two-party system and electoral college have failed on a systemic level.

Zs perceive the two-party system as destructive to democracy, with only 13 percent having confidence in the current political

---

128 Kim Parker and Ruth Igielnik, "What We Know about Gen Z So Far," Pew Research Center, February 9, 2021, https://www.pewresearch.org/social-trends/2020/05/14/on-the-cusp-of-adulthood-and-facing-an-uncertain-future-what-we-know-about-gen-z-so-far-2/.

system and only one in five saying they think they are living in a functioning democracy.[129]

Only 12 percent feel the two-party system is working:[130] the rest said it creates an insurmountable chasm, prevents collaboration, and undermines democracy. This negative view is underlined by the fact that an unprecedented share of Gen Z don't identify as either Republican or Democrat. A full one-third of Zs identify as independent,[131] even though the majority hold progressive positions that lean left.

Zs don't want to join a party, though. It's another box they don't want to check. They won't go us versus them, which is the very foundation of two-party politics.

A fourteen-year-old from North Carolina told us, "I don't want to be classified with either side. I have my own views, separate from a political party. Whatever I align with is based on my views, not a party's views. Being independent allows me to see issues from both sides rather than blindly digging in on one side for every issue."

As an aside, the more people that register as independent, the less support the two main parties will have, the less money they will raise, and the weaker their machines will become. As their whole operation is posited on being able to reach out to their respective bases, that could have profound consequences on the way we're accustomed to carrying out politics in this country.

---

129 Research by ZSpeak by Global Mosaic, November 2020.

130 Ibid.

131 Rishika Dugyala and Kamran Rahman, "6 Things to Know about Gen Z, Politics and 2020," Politico, October 11, 2020, https://www.politico.com/news/2020/10/11/gen-z-politics-2020-poll-takeaways-426767.

THE ELECTORAL COLLEGE

A twenty-year-old Z has witnessed two elections won by the loser of the popular vote: Bush in 2000 and Trump in 2016. In a third election, 2020, the loser tried to interfere with the electoral college through the courts, Congress, and ultimately, an armed invasion of the seat of government.

Twenty years, five presidential elections, and three victories dependent on the electoral college.

Even before the siege of Capitol Hill, Generation We was fully aware that our election system wasn't working. Think about it. If older generations had only lived through the last five elections, we would probably look at the system more critically, too.

Zs are impatient with institutions like the electoral college, so they're calling for change. That's their approach, identify a problem and address it, and that extends even to the US Constitution itself.

They don't see the Constitution as holy writ. "That's what the Constitution says" is an argument that doesn't work for them. Not on the Twelfth Amendment (the electoral college), not on the Second Amendment (the right to bear arms). They have little compunction about changing rules written by slave-owning, rich, White men 250 years ago that are palpably not working. How could the founders have known anything about our current gerrymandering or school shootings?

Generation We's attitude is simple: "If it doesn't work anymore, we have to change it."

There's no point in standing on ceremony.

A LIBERAL SHIFT

The oldest boomers started voting in 1964, so they were barely on the scene for the progressive landmarks of the '6os, such as the Civil Rights Act of 1964, the Voting Rights Act of 1965, Stonewall in 1969, or the first Earth Day in 1970. More came of voting age after Nixon's 1969 election, which began moving the United States back toward more conservative values that continued to gain momentum through the 1980s, when all boomers could vote. While the ideological spectrum produced Carter in 1977 and Clinton in 1993, boomer politics have leaned more conservative. And for more than four decades now, the boomers have driven our priority issues, formed the core vote of both parties, and provided most of our politicians.

The oldest Zs who voted for the first time in 2020 and tipped the election could be politically active until the turn of the next century. Some could vote in twenty general elections. Their impact on political priorities and the whole political system is just beginning.

The new shift toward progressive ideas began to show up in 2004, when the first millennials voted, and has intensified. Youth has been predominantly progressive and has voted predominantly Democrat. As the youth voting bloc continues to grow, its influence is increasing—and its progressiveness is intensifying. Youth are leading a shift in attitudes toward racial equity and criminal justice, immigration reform, gender rights, and climate change.

Youth is voting Democrat by margins unseen in the modern polling era. Since 2004, when the millennials could first vote en masse, the Democratic Party has won the popular youth vote in every midterm and presidential election. Previous generations, including Gen X, were more split. Ronald Reagan and George

W. Bush both won the youth vote for the Republicans. Bush and Gore split the youth vote equally in 2000. But in 2008, Barack Obama won the youth vote by thirty points, followed by Hillary Clinton by thirty points in 2016 (albeit with low voter turnout), and the Democrats by thirty-five points in the 2018 midterms.[132]

This trend is unprecedented. Those millennials who voted for the first time in 2004 are now entering their forties, with careers, homes, and established families—and they're still liberal. They voted for Biden in 2020. The youth vote is aging up with every year. This "youth" voting bloc is now aged eighteen into their early forties. By 2030, it will be ages eighteen to fifty.

And if anything, this sector of the voting population is becoming more liberal.

Everyone knows the popular stereotype that the liberal young inevitably become more conservative as they grow older, but political scientists actually find that once people's ideological leanings are determined in young adulthood, they don't tend to switch. If anything, they intensify and their ideological leanings become more pronounced with age. The boomers or Gen X who were moderate conservatives became more right-leaning over time. With this in mind, progressive millennials and Zs seem likely to lean further into their progressive views.

Of course, there are young Republicans. According to a 2020 Politico study, 20 percent of Gen Z identify as Republican,[133] as

---

132 David Faris, *The Kids Are All Left: How Young Voters Will Unite America* (Hoboken, NJ: Melville House Publishing, 2020).

133 Rishika Dugyala and Kamran Rahman, "6 Things to Know about Gen Z, Politics and 2020," Politico, October 11, 2020, https://www.politico.com/news/2020/10/11/gen-z-politics-2020-poll-takeaways-426767.

opposed to 35 percent of overall registered voters. That's much lower than it was in previous generations.

There aren't just fewer young Republicans; they're also a new sort of Republican because they're imbued with the common values of their generation. Pew Research found that Gen Z and millennial Republicans have more progressive views than older Republicans. In response to the question "Do you agree that Blacks aren't treated fairly?" only 20 percent of boomer Republicans agreed, as compared to 30 percent of millennial and 43 percent of Gen Z Republicans. Similarly, when researchers proposed the common Republican credo "The Earth is warming because of natural patterns rather than human activity," 42 percent of Republican boomers agreed, and 30 percent of millennials—but only 18 percent of Gen Z Republicans.[134]

In addition, there are the majority of Gen Z Republicans who believe in bigger government, rejecting a key plank of Republican orthodoxy.

Even though the majority of Zs lean left, they're going to change the nature of Republicanism.

Z Republicans are already closer in their beliefs to other Zs than to other Republicans, and they might change more. Given that most Zs are still minors, many have inherited their political views from their parents and may be growing up in heavily red communities (which skew rural). But young Zs are very mobile. Many will follow a trajectory from high school to some kind of

---

134 Kim Parker, Nikki Graf, and Ruth Igielnik, "Generation Z Looks a Lot like Millennials on Key Social and Political Issues," Pew Research Center, May 30, 2020, https://www.pewresearch.org/social-trends/2019/01/17/generation-z-looks-a-lot-like-millennials-on-key-social-and-political-issues/.

higher education and a move to a metro area for work. Their life paths will bring them to universities, cafés and bars, neighborhoods and block parties where progressive views are more prevalent. Current trends suggest that as one becomes more educated and/or more urban, one becomes more progressive.

FUTURE OF THE REPUBLICANS

In case it's not obvious by now, I could have titled this chapter "The Republicans Are Fucked."

If you look at the numbers, Republican voters are religiously affiliated White people over the age of forty-five. Gen Z and the millennials are largely non-White, under the age of forty-five, and less likely to have a religious affiliation.

One of those groups is growing; the other is slowly dying out. It's a numbers game.

When Zs look at the GOP, they barely recognize themselves. The same is true of the Democratic Party to some extent, too (the median age of members of Congress is sixty-seven, while the median age of their constituents is thirty-five), but Republican House members and senators tend to be older, more male, and whiter even than the Democrats. Gen Z looks at the GOP and doesn't see itself at all.

And even though Americans over the age of forty-five might be voting for at least another forty years, eventually the balance will tip.

What can Republicans do to resist this trend? Well, they're already doing some of it. They are gerrymandering electoral districts in their favor where they have the power to do so. During and after the 2020 election, they introduced measures that make it more difficult to vote early or by mail (incidentally, 70 percent of youth voted early or by mail in 2020).[135] In a thinly veiled response to 2020 BIPOC voter turnout, the GOP is now pushing for voter suppression laws in nearly all fifty states, intended to disproportionately impact these voters via stricter voter identification requirements—and even making it a criminal act to distribute water to voters waiting in line at the polls in largely BIPOC communities with notoriously long voter lines.

Ultimately, though, tinkering with voting procedures can only be a thumb in the dam. The only thing that will stop the decay of Republicanism is changing its position to appeal to young voters. That's liable to provoke howls of dismay from the Republican base, but that base is eroding day by day. Each time night falls over the great cities, the Midwest, the deserts, the mountains, and the coasts, a few more elderly Republicans leave the electoral rolls forever while a few more Zs enter. It's inexorable.

The Republicans are entrenched in pro-White, pro-religion positions that are fundamentally outdated. Religious affiliation is trending down sharply, especially among youth. Among the Silent Generation, 84 percent identify as Christian. Among the boomers, it's 76 percent, which is why it's been so important for Republicans to court the Christian vote. But of millennials, just 49 percent identify as Christian, while 35 percent identify as atheist, agnostic, or nothing.[136]

---

135 "Election Week 2020: Young People Increase Turnout, Lead Biden to Victory," CIRCLE at Tufts, November 25, 2020, https://circle.tufts.edu/latest-research/election-week-2020.

136 "In US, Decline of Christianity Continues at Rapid Pace," Pew Research Center, October 17, 2019, https://www.pewforum.org/2019/10/17/in-u-s-decline-of-christianity-continues-at-rapid-pace/.

That's nearly a 40 percent drop over three generations, and the trend is downward. There are no specific figures for Zs yet, but the majority of Gen Z—59 percent—say church is not important in their lives.[137]

Republicans are on the wrong side.

They're on the wrong side of the numbers on immigration, reproductive rights, and affordable healthcare—all touchstone issues for Generation We. And they're on the wrong side of science.

Zs' defining issue for the next century will be climate. In the early '90s, Newt Gingrich decided that Republican policy would be to deny climate change and global warming. They've stuck to that stance ever since. In 2021, this kind of denialism is a joke to any voter under the age of forty and to many over forty, too.

The Republicans traditionally tout a version of history in which the United States is the best country in the world for a whole range of reasons. When we asked Zs if they agreed that the United States was the best place in the world to live, a majority said no. Thanks to their digital access, they can see how people live in other parts of the world. The idea that America, with all its flaws, is exceptional makes no sense to them.

Nor does the idea that we need to return to some former greatness. Generation We didn't get the whole MAGA thing. They don't see how you can base a political philosophy on a return to greatness that never existed in the first place for most of their ancestors.

---

137 "Atheism Doubles among Generation Z," Barna Group, January 24, 2018, https://www.google.com/search?client=safari&rls=en&q=Atheism+Doubles+Among+Gene&ie=UTF-8&oe=UTF-8.

THE FUTURE OF THE DEMOCRATS

For all the omens of doom for the Republicans, the Democrats might be fucked, too.

Zs wanted to vote for Bernie Sanders in 2020, but he wasn't on the ballot, so they reluctantly settled for Joe Biden. In truth, Zs have as much trouble recognizing themselves in Sanders, Biden, or Nancy Pelosi as in the GOP (perhaps slightly less so with Sanders). But at least the Democrats speak the same language as the Zs—almost. The issues Zs say drove them to the polls in 2020—climate, racial justice, affordable healthcare, larger government, college debt—are all part of the Democrats' platform.

As we've seen, however, Zs may vote Democrat, but they over-whelming identify as independent. They are not the partisan Democrats the party has always relied on.

So the Democrats are in the same boat as the Republicans. Both sets of party grandees have worked on the assumption that new voters would simply climb aboard their platforms as they entered the electorate. In a world where Zs see even a purchase in a supermarket as casting a vote, imagine how much more discerning they're going to be about casting their actual votes.

Each party is going to have to work harder to earn support.

Zs don't think the current Democratic Party goes far enough to the left. They think Biden should have embraced the Green New Deal, even though polling suggests that would probably have lost him the election in 2020 (Zs are no less prone to political idealism and naïveté as any other generation at their age). Zs also criticize Democrats for being soft on criminal justice reform, mainly because the party has resisted their calls to defund or reform the police. Again, there's evidence that this move could alienate many older Democratic voters.

Generation We does, however, identify with the fact that there are more diverse members in the Democratic Party. In particular, they point to the Squad, four left-leaning BIPOC women in the House who are defiant in breaking down barriers to representation: Alexandria Ocasio-Cortez (better known as AOC), Ilhan Omar, Ayanna Pressley, and Rashida Tlaib. Zs heavily follow AOC in particular, who was just twenty-nine when she was elected. Ilhan Omar ended a 181-year-old ban when she became the first person ever to wear a head covering on the floor of the House. Her seventeen-year-old daughter, Isra Hirsi, was one of the co-founders of the US Youth Climate Strike and has been named in *Fortune*'s 40 under 40 in Government and Politics.

The Squad notwithstanding, most Democrats are operating from a more moderate platform than their Z voting constituents. They might have to move to the left to maintain support, or to counter a Republican move toward the middle. Generation We would be happy with that. With the youth vote growing, smart money could be on a far-left liberal like AOC for president in another decade or so.

If the Democrats don't move far or fast enough on climate, in particular, a write-in candidate could appear on the left or the Green Party could gain momentum. The same might happen with defunding or reforming the police, which is hugely divisive between generations. A third-party candidate would likely fail—none has received more than 5.7 percent of the vote in any election since 2000[138]—but the Democrats could be doomed if left-leaning voters are split.

And *that's* how Republicans could get elected again in defiance of all the numbers.

TAKING UP THE REINS

Youth are throwing their hat in the political ring at much younger ages than generations before in order to achieve more diverse representation and propel their solutions forward. Millennials and the oldest Zs are involved in campaigns and state and local races. The executive director of the American Association of Political Consultants says that 15 percent of their members are under thirty, and that percentage is growing. These young political consultants are particularly passionate about being involved in campaigns to get women, BIPOC, and LGBTQ+ candidates elected.

The US Constitution forbids candidates younger than twenty-five and thirty for the House and Senate, respectively. That rules the Zs out—for now. But youth are getting an earlier start by running for positions in state legislature: in 2018, 700 millennials ran for state legislative seats. And as they age up, they turn their sights higher: in 2020, 259 millennials ran for congressional seats alone.[139]

In Wisconsin, nineteen-year-old Kalan Haywood became the

---

138 Aaron O'Neill, "U.S. Presidential Elections: Third-Party Performance 1892–2020," Statista, February 17, 2021, https://www.statista.com/statistics/1134513/third-party-performance-us-elections/.

139 Esha Sarai, "Record Numbers of Millennials Run for Public Office," Voice of America, November 2, 2020, https://www.voanews.com/2020-usa-votes/record-numbers-millennials-run-public-office.

youngest member of his state legislature when he was inaugurated, having run his campaign as a high school senior. As a Black Z, he was compelled to enter politics to address issues like unemployment and mass incarceration that disproportionately affect BIPOC. Cassandra Levesque was a Girl Scout when she started working on issues around child marriage, which pushed her into formal politics. She became the youngest member of her House in New Hampshire, again at the age of nineteen. Meanwhile, the first Gen Z legislator in California, Alex Lee, is Asian and openly bisexual. He supports universal healthcare, racial justice, and tuition-free college and was arrested in June 2020 while protesting for police reform with his peers.

Black school kids, Girl Scouts, and bisexual Asians—this is the future face of Z representation.

Z Voices

EVAN MALBROUGH: THE ORGANIZER

Twenty-three-year-old Evan Malbrough (he/him) is a Georgia native, honors graduate of Georgia State University, founder of the Georgia Youth Poll Worker Project, author, and advocate for voter rights.

Q: Why do you think youth today are so engaged in politics compared with previous generations?

A: Access to information. We were bombarded with all of this programming and given access to all of this information, which made us more adept at entering into activism, organizing, and having a higher awareness of social issues that are affecting our community and our country.

Q: How did you feel about the voter turnout numbers in 2020?

A: They were phenomenal. One in five people who voted in Georgia were young people. I did an interview on MSNBC and they tweeted that I said, "Gen Z is the largest voting bloc and we should be treated with respect because we will carry whatever party we get behind." I remember the Twitter responses from older people that said, "Well, they don't vote." So I think that put that stereotype to rest and really helped establish young people as a constituency rather than just a gamble or something not worth investing in.

Q: Can you expand more on what you mean by young people as a constituency?

A: Politicians these days treat young people as a constituency to be managed, while they treat older populations as a constituency to be served. If you look at the boomer or silent generations, their concerns are seen as more valid that politicians cater to. They say to the boomer generation, "We're going to do these policies to get your vote, base our polling and our future action on your opinions," while they look at Gen Z as more of a constituency to be managed. There's a stereotype that we are disillusioned, that we don't know about the systems we inhabit. And now it's up to the political class to actually draft policies that cater to us, as they have done for generations before.

Q: How are Zs' demands of government different?

A: The social contract. Boomers were able to build the systems they got rich off of and their relationship with governance is very secure. Boomers want to conserve the systems they benefit from. We're trying to renegotiate that contract, because the more and more of us are able to vote, the more leverage we have to change that social contract. I think that's something that's causing a lot of friction between the generations.

Q: Why is there so much difference between older and younger generations in their priorities and sense of progress?

A: Our experiences are different. My parents were born in the '60s before the Civil Rights Act, so they lived in a pretty racialized society. My grandparents lived in segregation. My grandfather was a sharecropper. There's a different idea of progress when you're born in the segregated South versus coming up in 2021. The events that define you: Bloody Sunday or the March on Washington or the Birmingham church bombing versus the things that affected our generation, like the Trayvon Martin shooting, the Michael Brown shooting. I think I might have been one or two when the Los Angeles riots happened. I barely have a reference for 9/11 either. When you have these different lenses that define your life, your idea of progress is totally different.

Q: What's the one belief or system that needs to change to move us forward in politics?

A: The idea of representation. We need to give elected officials less power. And give people more of a say. Going back to what George Washington said, the two parties went rampant, and it's to the detriment of everybody. We're seeing the representatives are just representing themselves. And now it's to the detriment of their own voting bodies.

Q: Where do you feel like you, personally, can make the most impact at this point?

A: I am working to open a center for democratic organizing at my alma mater, GSU. Potential names are the Southern Center for Democratic Organizing or the Good Trouble Center for Democratic Organizing, because it's in John Lewis's district down the street from his Atlanta office. I want to help create an environment for college-age organizers and future civic leaders to receive training and resources to grow into the leaders we need. Our hope is that the center will provide classes, scholarships, and fellowships to do just that.

CHAPTER 11

Hacking Life

"There are so many different ways to create a career for your-self in today's society that does not require a formal education. Although education is still important, there are many different things you can do without it. You can become an influencer, you can create things online, you can do a trade. Everyone has talents that they can use to create a career for themselves, some just might take a little more creativity than others."

—SEVENTEEN-YEAR-OLD Z, MASSACHUSETTS

Cami Tellez was twenty-two when she dropped out of college to create an underwear company, dismayed by the dominance of brands such as Victoria's Secret that she saw as nonethical (reliant on sweatshops and prison labor) and perpetuating beauty as thin, White, and cisgender. In response, Tellez created a disruptive company that's sustainable, inclusive, and body positive and soon found a market among Zs who shared her values.

Founded in fall 2019, Tellez's company, Parade, had sold 700,000 pairs of underwear and brought in $10 million in revenue by late 2020. Tellez said, "Parade has been able to create a groundswell, a cultural zeitgeist. I think that we're changing the way a whole generation of women see themselves, and I think that's why we've been so successful." Underscoring the power of this movement, Parade estimates that one in eight of their customers has posted a picture of themselves in the underwear online.

Tellez is never going to finish college. She's hacked her life.

Tellez isn't the only college dropout to achieve business success, and the phenomenon didn't start with Generation We, but more and more Zs are finding ways to hack traditional approaches to work and to education, too.

There are two reasons for this. One is generational: Zs are independent and creative and highly purposeful in nature. They want to forge their own paths. The second is driven by necessity...or desperation. Zs can see that neither a traditional education nor career necessarily offer a path to success. A twenty-one-year-old from Georgia told us, "I definitely think we're at a point where people are realizing traditional education is kind of a joke. Of course we still need lawyers and doctors and other occupations where school is necessary, but some people go through all that schooling and end up having to work a fast food job when the economy crashes. It's not guaranteed success. There is an influx in entrepreneurs, and no one wants to work a typical nine-to-five that they do not enjoy."

Generation We has grown up watching its immediate successors, the millennials, be failed by the traditional systems. They've seen older siblings or cousins in their young adulthood moving back to their hometowns, sleeping on their parents' basement futons, and endlessly applying to jobs. They've had their Grubhub delivered by college graduates.

Twenty- and thirty-somethings with masters' degrees are picking them up in Ubers.

Zs don't want to follow a path that only leads to college debt and an uncertain future.

It comes back to their habitual realism. Millennials were more idealistic, at a time when the culture still embraced that traditional trajectory of high school leads to higher ed leads to a good, stable job. That linear path was blown up for millennials due to roller-coaster economics, a "hire and fire" corporate culture, and a shift to the contract or gig economy. Millennials believed, even as they racked up tons of college debt, the job market would be there for them to earn it back. It wasn't.

Generation We are now more realistic; in addition, as we've seen, they are accustomed to being creators. They feel empowered to create their own lives instead of following a prescribed linear path. One sixteen-year-old in Florida told us, "There are many other ways to create a career in today's world with the internet and social media. Now more than ever, people can make money by not going to school and enjoying what they do rather than conform to a certain criteria on how to become something."

Jake Doolittle is a twenty-year-old photographer and video creator for TikTokers, YouTubers, and musicians. At sixteen, he fell in love with photography, and when he couldn't afford tickets to music concerts, he would email the manager and offer to shoot the concert in exchange for attendance. As he says, "I was like sixteen and I had no clue what I was doing. I shot for a band when they came into Portland. And then after that it was Billie Eilish. I just got so lucky that I found Billie at a hundred thousand followers. I jumped on it, and she was at a five hundred capacity venue. And then the next I shot for her was six thousand people. I just feel like if you believe that your success or other people's success is going to go a certain way, you keep pursuing it. And then it sort of took off from there."

Did it ever. In the past year, Jake has worked with Charli D'Amelio (the #1 TikToker) and *Saturday Night Live.* He completed community college but is now focusing on his work as a creator versus pursuing a four-year degree. "I think for certain people, [college] is great in certain industries. For me, community college was helpful to go and figure myself out. I feel I know what I want to do. I completely understand the risks and I believe that I am going to succeed no matter what. I love the feeling of working my ass off. It's the best. I'm just focused on the goal and I love it."

As realists, Zs expect that they'll have to work hard to get wherever they're going. They don't expect instant success as a creator, influencer, or entrepreneur. Zs are not afraid of *work*. In the words of a twenty-three-year-old from Illinois: "Colleges are mongering more and more dollars from the younger generation, setting up a future with overwhelming debt, which is extremely concerning. There are many alternatives for success these days that aren't a traditional degree. The common misconception is that these opportunities come easily. Just as you put work into college studies, these opportunities require just as much work, but hopefully you are passionate enough about them to pursue them to the fullest."

One of Stanford's most popular classes among Zs is called Designing Your Life. It shows students how to apply engineering design principles to their own lives: identify the purpose, the benefits, and the barriers, then use your imagination to create something new and innovative. The creators are both Silicon Valley veterans who have now written a book based on the popularity of the class. Other universities are replicating similar courses that enable and encourage Zs to figure out their passions and how to achieve them.

For the most creative generation, the ultimate act of creation is to create their own life.

Two-thirds of Zs hope to be entrepreneurs of some kind,[140] marrying together entrepreneurialism and purpose. There have never been so many role models to follow. While millennials looked to the pioneers in Silicon Valley, Gen Z prefers disruptors like Elon Musk. Musk is not "just" an entrepreneur; he's a social environmental disruptor who wants to remake the world in his own vision, and it goes way beyond his electric cars to battery storage and solar to carbon capture and SpaceX. That's very appealing to Zs. As a twenty-three-year-old from California said, "Elon Musk is someone I look up to. He prioritizes innovative change in our tech world as well as positive change in our environment. He has also emphasized many times that not having a degree doesn't necessarily mean you aren't intelligent."

For a lot of Zs looking up to creators and influencers, their parents might be the only people they know who work a traditional nine-to-five job. When we asked Zs if they'd prefer to be a creator or have a traditional job, most responded, "What's a traditional job anymore?"

Nearly every Z is doing something more entrepreneurial. They have their own hustle.

---

140 Research by ZSpeak by Global Mosaic, May 2021.

Unlike millennials and previous generations, Zs are not driven solely by money. Like Musk, they are more likely to think, "I don't see what I want to see in the world, so I'm going to create it." This often involves solving some kind of social or environmental problem.

A large majority of Zs—87 percent—say that success is doing work that matches your passion.[141] They want to do something that feels purposeful. A twenty-two-year-old in Florida told us, "A successful career is doing good in the world and making positive changes, not just to your bank account."

THE PROBLEM WITH HIGHER EDUCATION

For decades, there has been an accepted progression from high school to higher education to career (for those who could afford it). That whole progression is under threat because its central stage, residential higher education, no longer offers the same value proposition it used to.

For a long time, a college degree was a direct predictor of increased future earnings.

Not anymore.

Even the *Harvard Business Review* has acknowledged that there are faster and cheaper pathways to getting a good first job than a slow, expensive bachelor's degree.[142] In fact, it could be argued that for some time, committing to a four-year res-

---

141 "Helping Students Succeed," ECMC Group—News, March 2020, https://www.ecmcgroup.org/news.html.

142 Ryan Craig, "Will a Bachelor's Degree Matter as Much for Gen Z?" *Harvard Business Review*, October 7, 2019, https://hbr.org/2019/10/will-a-bachelors-degree-matter-as-much-for-gen-z.

idential bachelor's degree has not been as much a *rational* choice as an *emotional* one: going to the "right" college is an important status symbol, as recent college admissions scandals underscore.

The value proposition for higher education started changing with the millennials, but they didn't realize that until it was too late. Around half—49 percent—now say their degree is virtually irrelevant to their current job,[143] and only about 27 percent of college graduates work in a field related to their degree.[144]

It's doubly ironic. Millennials are the most highly educated generation, but their economic trajectory is way below that of previous generations. And the education that failed to improve their economic chances also cost them more than it did the generations before them.

Only about 40 percent of college students who start a degree complete it,[145] and of those who do, only 53 percent gain employment straight out of college.[146] The Bureau for Economic Research estimates that more than 40 percent of recent gradu-

143 James Wellemeyer, "Half of Young Americans Say Their Degree Is Irrelevant to Their Work," MarketWatch, August 11, 2019, https://www.marketwatch.com/story/half-of-young-americans-say-college-isnt-necessary-2019-08-06.

144 Brad Plumer, "Only 27 Percent of College Grads Have a Job Related to Their Major," *The Washington Post*, May 20, 2013, https://www.washingtonpost.com/news/wonk/wp/2013/05/20/only-27-percent-of-college-grads-have-a-job-related-to-their-major/.

145 Valerie Strauss, "'A Dereliction of Duty': The College Dropout Scandal—and How to Fix It," *The Washington Post*, September 10, 2019, https://www.washingtonpost.com/education/2019/09/10/a-dereliction-duty-college-dropout-scandal-how-fix-it/.

146 "What Can Students Do to Improve Their Chances of Finding Employment after College?" DO-IT, April 9, 2021, https://www.washington.edu/doit/what-can-students-do-improve-their-chances-finding-employment-after-college.

ates are underemployed in their first job. And half of those will still be underemployed a decade later.[147]

That wasn't true for boomers and Gen X, but it's what Zs see when they look at millennials.

The pandemic only made things worse. In the 2020 and 2021 academic years, Zs or their older siblings or friends paid up to $70,000 to go to top schools, only to sit in their bedroom doing remote learning. Many wondered if the price would be worth it even if they were on campus. Why sign up to a system that's broken?

In 2020, US student debt reached $1.6 trillion, second only to housing debt and $0.5 trillion more than all US credit card debt combined. A decade earlier, that figure was $600 billion, so half of the explosion in student debt has taken place after Zs started going to college.[148]

The average college student graduates with $37,000 of debt.[149] But this is the *mean*. Consider that affluent students often don't need to take on any debt, which means that for many poorer or middle-class students, the level of debt is actually a lot higher than this average.

Generation We is terrified of being saddled with so much debt at such a young age: 82 percent say college debt will affect their

147 "The Labor Market for Recent College Graduates," Federal Reserve Bank of New York, December 2021, https://www.newyorkfed.org/research/college-labor-market/index.html.

148 "Student Loans Owned and Securitized, Outstanding," FRED, February 5, 2021, https://fred.stlouisfed.org/series/SLOAS.

149 Allison Wignall, "Student Loan Debt in America Is $1.3 Trillion: How Much Is That Exactly," College Raptor Blog, August 31, 2020, https://www.collegeraptor.com/paying-for-college/articles/questions-answers/americas-student-loan-debt-1-3-trillion-much-exactly-infographic/.

major life decisions, like whether they'll have to give up grad school or purchase a home. The *New York Post* asked millennials about the impact of student debt, and 43 percent said that buying a house was a financial impossibility (23 percent said they had to live with their parents) and the same number said they couldn't save for retirement. Almost 40 percent said they need some kind of side hustle to help meet debt repayments, and about a third of Zs said they don't feel able to get married or consider starting a family while they have such levels of debt.[150]

One of the big reasons Zs loved Bernie Sanders in 2020 was his policy that higher education should be free and all college debt should be canceled to give young people the best hand up (President Biden began his administration considering debt forgiveness). It's one of the biggest sources of stress in Zs' lives.

The *New York Post* also offered students various options to assess the lengths they would go to to cancel college debt. Around 40 percent said they'd be willing to give up caffeine for good, and about the same number that they'd spend a week in jail. Just over 51 percent said they would be prepared to shave their head to cancel their debt.[151]

It was millennials and their boomer parents who drove the competition among colleges over the last twenty years to build the fanciest dorms and the best workout facilities, hiking costs skyward. Zs entered the market at the high point, already questioning the ROI (return on investment). They began to swing the pendulum back toward value for money. As a twenty-three-

---

150 Allison Sadlier, "Most College Grads Consider Their Student Debt a Life Sentence," *New York Post*, November 1, 2019, https://nypost.com/2019/11/01/most-college-grads-consider-their-student-debt-a-life-sentence/.

151 Ibid.

year-old in California told us, "COVID has shifted everyone's value systems about everything. With more students being rejected from colleges due to occupancy restrictions, I think it will force us all to reconsider the enormous price we pay for a bachelor's degree with very little promise of return on the investment."

ALTERNATIVE PATHS

So Zs are disrupting the conventional education path. One study found that 89 percent of Gen Z have considered not going straight into a four-year degree from high school. About one-third of those planning to go to college thought about taking a gap year instead to acquire the specific skills they need to do the kind of work they want to do.[152]

Changing college demographics bear this out. About one-third of US college students are now over the age of twenty-five. Necessity has driven people to fit education into their lives differently. Many work for several years first; about half of full-time students work simultaneously to being in school. There are more online, hybrid, weekend, and evening classes, more certifications, and more schools combining in-class instruction with real-world experience, where internships, research, or work are part of the degree. There are more non-four-year-degree programs and boot camps that lead directly to digital jobs, run by companies such as Adobe, Google, and Microsoft.

There's also a returning trend toward technical education (what used to be called trade school) and apprenticeships, learning

---

152 James Wellemeyer, "Half of Young Americans Say Their Degree Is Irrelevant to Their Work," MarketWatch, August 11, 2019, https://www.marketwatch.com/story/half-of-young-americans-say-college-isnt-necessary-2019-08-06.

on the job like generations of workers did in the past. Such a career-based or hands-on approach appeals to Zs, as do the economics: they get paid for learning.

PERSONALIZE YOUR STUDIES

Zs are also changing what they want to study. With many employers complaining about a digital skills gap, Zs are set to benefit, leveraging their native skills with a rise in digital majors. We also see a rise in environmental science studies, as well as more colleges and universities converting business degrees into green business degrees and sustainable business degrees, and a growth in degrees around entrepreneurship. That seems counterintuitive, as people tend to perceive entrepreneurs as functioning outside of any kind of system that can be taught, but three-quarters of Zs want colleges to teach entrepreneurship,[153] although plenty others say they can best learn this in the real world.

Again, the creative generation wants to personalize what they learn: three-quarters of Zs are interested in designing their own major.[154] Guess what? Zs don't want to fit into existing molds. (Remember, they hate to check the prescribed boxes.) Driven by Zs' individual interests and the merging of industries, we're seeing lots of new mash-ups. The University of Southern California, for example, created the Iovine and Young Academy, a mash-up of art and design, technology and engineering, and marketing and business to allow students to create their own

153 Jeffrey J. Selingo, "The New Generation of Students: How Colleges Can Recruit, Teach, and Serve Gen Z," *The Chronicle of Higher Education*, 2018, http://connect.chronicle.com/rs/931-EKA-218/images/NextGenStudents_ExecutiveSummary_v5%20_2019.pdf.

154 Elaina Loveland, "Instant Generation," National Association for College Admissions Counseling, 2021, https://www.nacacnet.org/news--publications/journal-of-college-admission/instant-generation/.

paths. Other schools are creating business incubators and accelerators that leverage Zs' creativity and entrepreneurial spirit.

Even physical learning spaces are evolving for Gen Z.

That's important because even though a lot more education is sure to happen online, research suggests that 57 percent of Zs still say that they prefer in-person activities with classmates.[155] Remote learning through the pandemic made them miss in-classroom collaboration even more. As a twenty-year-old from Idaho told us, "After COVID, being able to actually go to class physically, I won't take an 8:00 a.m. for granted again."

To attract Zs, colleges and universities are investing in flexible, collaborative learning spaces, with nontraditional lighting and modular furniture that can be adapted for different purposes— as well as makerspaces, fabrication labs, and digital labs—to encourage creativity and collaboration. Zs we've talked to prioritize collaborative spaces over five-star dormitories.

When selecting their college, Zs look beyond academic rankings to rankings on diversity. They look to see if schools have student communities that serve minorities and LGBTQ+. Just as they've experienced on TikTok, Zs know an educational experience will be richer when filled with a broader range of people and perspectives. As a twenty-three-year-old in Rhode Island said, "It's important that a college is an inclusive space for all people of every background, race, political views, and orientation or identity. Being inclusive of all people and all their ideas is an important part of academic development for society as a whole." Many Zs may not consider a school that doesn't fit these requirements, like this

---

155 "Rethinking Training and Development for Generation Z," Panopto Video Platform, July 22, 2020, https://www.panopto.com/blog/rethinking-training-and-development-for-generation-z/.

seventeen-year-old from Ohio: "As a person of color, I would want to see other people who look like me. I also believe anyone of any sexual orientation or race should be treated like everybody else, so if I saw a college or campus that wasn't very inclusive, then I would definitely think to myself about what they really stand for."

Just as Zs are challenging the power structure in other aspects of society, so too at their colleges and universities. They expect a seat at the table. In the past, students were passive, accepting the authority of school administrators, but Zs have strong ideas on the culture and content of their educational experience. They expect to be involved actors with agency and voice in the decisions made within the administration.

They have brought their activism to campus, standing up against university cover-ups of sexual violence on campus, echoing the #MeToo movement and demanding greater accountability from their administrations, as shown in the 2015 documentary *The Hunting Ground*, about sexual assaults on campus. They've spoken out and petitioned against professors, guest speakers, and even university presidents they perceive as representing anti-Islam, anti-Semitic, sexist, or racist ideas.

While older generations battle over the "liberalization" of higher education (some American conservatives see English classes requiring reading from BIPOC and Indigenous authors, alongside Shakespeare and Plato, as a harbinger of the downfall of Western civilization), Zs want to be part of the discussion on what is taught in higher education. On which texts are deemed important or legitimate. Their goal is not to limit, as it is often perceived, but instead to represent a *broader* range of perspectives than ever before. One twenty-three-year-old in California said, "I feel it's important that students have the power. A college can't consider themselves progressive without giving marginalized voices actual agency and power."

It's safe to say that schools have to think more like Zs.

THE WORLD OF WORK

Traditional salaried jobs are declining, with a shift toward a contract and gig economy.

Among millennials, 40 percent have a bachelor's degree (it was only 26 percent for boomers and 32 percent for Gen X),[156] but those millennials can't achieve the same economic self-sufficiency as boomers and Gen X because traditional stable jobs are not as plentiful as they once were. It's only going to be more difficult for Zs because the gig economy is the death knell of employees in the traditional sense.

Zs see work as a hustle they have to put together through multiple jobs or contracts. Asking someone "What do you do?" is not as simple anymore. Zs want to know your side hustle, too, because everyone has one. A Z may be doing a bunch of stuff at once: school, plus an internship or apprenticeship, plus a Depop or Etsy shop, plus paid content on TikTok, YouTube, or Twitch.

The gig economy is the primary source of income for more than a half (53 percent) of Americans aged eighteen to thirty-four, which includes Zs plus the younger millennials.[157]

---

156 Nikki Graf, "More Young Workers than Ever Are College Grads in US," Pew Research Center, July 27, 2020, https://www.pewresearch.org/fact-tank/2017/05/16/todays-young-workers-are-more-likely-than-ever-to-have-a-bachelors-degree/.

157 "The Gig Economy," Edison Research, Marketplace, December 2018, http://www.edisonresearch.com/wp-content/uploads/2019/01/Gig-Economy-2018-Marketplace-Edison-Research-Poll-FINAL.pdf.

Zs are somewhat conflicted about the gig economy. Most say they love being their own boss and value the flexibility of their own schedule. No wonder, because the dream for most Zs is to be a creator, and it's thrilling to put one's passion out into the world and make money at it. At the same time, they're concerned about the gig economy's lack of stability, unpredictable pay, and lack of healthcare and benefits.

As Jake Doolittle (the photographer and video creator) reflected, "It's difficult. I tell people, 'You're not going to get any work for the first three to six months.' I would say for each email that I've gotten a reply to, I was sending five hundred emails. If you want to do this for a living, you have to be a risk taker. You can definitely fall in the slums where you don't get work for a month and it feels awful. One month I'll be working for the biggest TikToker in the world, and then the next week I will be selling most of my closet to try to make ends meet. Stuff can fall through."

So Zs are hacking work for the same reasons they're hacking education: partly because they're creative and independent, and partly because they have little choice.

Combining multiple gig jobs can enable a more fluid lifestyle but often with less reward. Fewer Zs expect to purchase real estate or a car, partly because the lack of stable work prevents them from being able to afford it.

The COVID pandemic of 2020 brought another swerve to the job trajectories of Generation We as they were going into or attending university, preparing for internships, or to enter the job market. Unemployment for Zs went from 8.4 percent in April, May, and June 2019 to 24.4 percent after the pandemic,[158] and 64 percent had their internships canceled and were not offered compensation.[159] They couldn't work for a year and a half. No one knows how much more difficult that will make their working lives in the future.

Some Zs are already making their names in business at a very young age. Trey Brown was a twelve-year-old self-described hustler when he used his birthday money to found SPERGO, a boutique fashion brand. Two years later, he was loaned $25,000 by Sean Combs to grow the business. Maxine Marcus was a high school sophomore when she did an internship with a company and enthralled her employers by how savvy she was on social media. They hired her as a marketing social media strategist at fifteen. She then pitched another company to run their in-house research program building out apps for Zs. By her senior year, Maxine founded AmbassCo to bridge the gap between business executives and Gen Z, inviting companies to test market strategies on high schoolers and college students. She's leveraged her digital and social media knowledge to hack the world of work.

OFFICES AND BEYOND

As is the case for many Americans post-COVID, there is evidence that Zs' geography is changing as well. In past generations, young job seekers flocked to big cities like New York, Chicago, LA, or San Francisco. Zs seem to be different.

They're pragmatists, after all. With the disentanglement of work

---

158 Megan Leonhardt, "Job Losses Hit Gen Z Harder during the Pandemic than Older Generations," CNBC, October 15, 2020, https://www.cnbc.com/2020/10/15/gen-z-more-vulnerable-to-job-losses-during-the-pandemic.html.

159 Akala Adedayo, "Students among Workers Getting Stiffed as Many Internships Canceled. Here's How They Can Stay Competitive," CNBC, April 24, 2020, https://www.cnbc.com/2020/04/22/64percent-of-canceled-job-internships-offer-no-compensation.html.

from physical space and the lack of a regular, predictable salary, Zs are joining the general shift from major cities to secondary markets. It's hard to live in a big metro if you're a gig worker. And if you're working online, you can live wherever you want.

According to a recent Glassdoor analysis, Gen Z job applications are less concentrated in the big metros and instead spread among smaller cities like Frisco in Texas, Nolensville in Tennessee, Scottsdale in Georgia, and so on.[160] Nice places, manageable places, good places to live.

The traditional office might not be dead after the pandemic recedes, but Zs want to be able to have some say in where and when they want to work. One-third of Zs say that they would not work for an employer who gave them no say over their work schedule.[161]

The hashtag #CottageCore became a runaway trend among Zs during lockdown, with more than 6 billion views on TikTok. It's full of beautiful meadows and people baking bread or picking flowers, celebrating a simpler lifestyle. This hashtag might represent nothing more than escapism and rural romanticism, but it might also impact future lifestyle decisions if Zs trapped in cities are longing for a simpler lifestyle outside the city.

Perhaps you couldn't blame them for wanting to escape. As we're about to see, Gen Z spend their lives under a lot of pressure.

---

160 Amanda Stansell, "The Next Generation of Talent: Where Gen Z Wants to Work," Glassdoor Economic Research, February 20, 2019, https://www.glassdoor.com/research/gen-z-workers/#.

161 Dana Wilkie, "Generation Z Says They Work the Hardest, but Only When They Want To," SHRM, August 16, 2019, https://www.shrm.org/resourcesandtools/hr-topics/employee-relations/pages/gen-z-worries-about-work-skills.aspx.

Z Voices

TIFFANY ZHONG: THE CREATOR

Tiffany Zhong (she/her) dropped out of Berkley as a sophomore and by the age of twenty-three had created two companies (Zebra IQ and Islands) and was the youngest venture capitalist in the United States. She is a *Forbes* 30 under 30, on *Vanity Fair*'s Future Innovators Index, and an Adweek Young Influential.

Q: You became a creator and entrepreneur at such a young age. Where did that come from?

A: I was in middle school using Facebook, and my dad was, like, "Instead of being a person addicted to these products, you should be the one building products that people are using." I started thinking, is there any way I can build things myself? What does that look like? How can I learn from people who have built cool things?

Q: Millennials are creative for sure, but they're more digital consumers, whereas I feel Zs are digital creators. Why do you think that is?

A: Zs realize they can make content, and technological advancements make it so easy for us to make content, to make websites, to build things ourselves. With the simplicity and usability of these new tools that let us make videos from our smartphones in five seconds, that has created a whole generation of creators, whether for fun or to drive a personal mission. There's the power of Twitter, the power of TikTok. One tweet can go viral and can change your whole life.

Q: What motivates you to create and run your own business?

A: I want to set a precedent for future generations that what I do is possible. I want to use content, social media, and my businesses to inspire 100 million people to realize they can live their best life and help them get to that, whatever that may be...You're not limited by who you are anymore. You're not limited by anything.

Q: How do Zs think about work differently from older generations?

A: Zs turn their hobbies into a side hustle, figuring out how to turn what they're interested in doing and monetizing it or building a brand around it. So it's kind of a win-win. The question I always think about is, what feels like play to you? A lot of people are forced into figuring out a major in college and force themselves into a certain profession, sinking themselves into debt and maybe can't even find a job.

Q: How do you feel about the relevance of a traditional education?

A: High school wasn't really for me. College wasn't really for me. I learn best by actually jumping in as opposed to learning by textbook. But that's me. That's also tied to the work I do, which is building tech companies, building media companies. I don't necessarily need a college education for these things. There's a lot I can learn online or from people in those spaces directly. That's the best hacky way of navigating your career, navigating your life. We're going to move toward a world where it's going to be a very personalized experience for each kid. It's not going to just be one path where everyone is forced into going to high school or going to college.

Q: What other characteristics do young people have today besides just knowing how to create?

A: Entrepreneurial risk-taking. This generation is less afraid to do things.

Q: What's your vision for the future of the creator economy?

A: My prediction is that in ten years, these creator businesses are going to be the next *Fortune* 500 companies. Examples are the Kylie Jenner empire, the Mr. Beast empire, and a lot of YouTubers like Charli D'Amelio's empire, as well as music artists who make the right business moves. It's really about owning equity in businesses as opposed to just doing endorsement deals.

Q: What's the main thing that needs to be deconstructed in our culture to unleash the full potential of the creator economy?

A: The respect from people over forty who are still, like, how is this a job? How much can you actually make from doing this? Right. You can make a lot of money being a creator. It's funny because people like Elon Musk, he's his own personality. They're not just building companies. They're also building their own brand.

So it's entrepreneurs becoming creators, creators becoming entrepreneurs, investors becoming creators, creators becoming investors: the world is converging between entertainment and business. This can be a full-time job. Yeah, 100 percent. Not only that. I would encourage everyone to be a creator.

Q: What's the one thing you want people to know?

A: You only need 500 superfans to be able to make a living online.

CHAPTER 12

The Gen Z Burden

"I'm borderline between burnout and anxiety. Like there is only so much you can say and there's only so much that your voice is doing and sometimes you just wish you could do more and solve a lot of these, like bigger issues that need to be solved right away."

—EIGHTEEN-YEAR-OLD Z, DELAWARE

Any conflict takes a terrible toll on the combatants: ongoing fear, effort, stress, and danger leave them with shell shock, with a thousand-yard stare, with PTSD.

That's what's happening now to our young people. There's a price to pay for spending their lives with a front-row seat to all that is broken in our world.

Generation We didn't ask to take on so much responsibility at such a young age and they're suffering for it. You can hear them describe the mounting stress they feel. An eighteen-year-old from Minnesota told us, "My dream job wasn't to be an activist. It's a burden we've had to take on, and fortunately we've found passion in it and in wanting to change our communities for the better. But none of us wanted to be here.

We kind of felt like we had to be here and take on this role because nobody else was."

This is the Gen Z burden.

I strongly believe that Gen Z will improve the world for everyone, and I feel equally strongly that we need to take care of them.

The Gen Z burden is the result of a perfect storm of critical issues reaching an inflection point, Zs coming of age, and their digital connectivity and awareness.

It stole their innocence and gave them a sense of responsibility that's been weighing them down since elementary school. That's the flip side of their activism.

Generation We didn't choose any of this; they didn't volunteer to try to reshape the world. They would have liked to have been carefree kids or teenagers like previous generations, walking to the park instead of in rallies, shouting in backyards instead of at corporate leaders, gathering at concerts instead of at government buildings (of course, the constant threat of gun violence compromises even the most innocent of these activities today).

Greta Thunberg voiced their resentments at age sixteen, when addressing world leaders at the United Nations: "How dare you, you have stolen my dreams and my childhood. We are not the ones who are responsible for this, but we are the ones who will have to live out the consequences. That is so incredibly unfair."

GENERATIONAL TRAUMA

Trauma is different for different generations. The poster issue for millennials was bullying. Terms like "cyberbullying" were invented to combat the new era of digital interactions and the new kind of stress it inflicted on that generation. Bullying was real but also had a very clear cause and effect and, in many cases, a simple remedy like telling a teacher.

For Generation We, the issues are of a different level of complexity and consequence. The future of the climate can't be solved by telling a teacher or through an after-school special. It weighs on Zs as an ongoing form of internalized anxiety and depression.

Zs also face more specific, direct threats. In 2020, the American Psychological Association's (APA's) annual study *Stress in America* identified gun violence as the top source of stress for Generation We: 72 percent of Zs say they're stressed about school shootings.[162]

That's not the world boomers grew up in, or Xs, or even millennials. It's not the world of *Leave It to Beaver* or *The Breakfast Club*, or even *Buffy the Vampire Slayer*. Since 2009, there have been more than180 school shootings in the United States.[163] This is a world where parents send their kids to school with their lunchboxes and a reminder that "if anything happens, I love you." A film by that name won the 2021 Oscar for Short Animated Film, about two grieving parents who lost their daughter to a school shooting. As a parent of two school-aged daughters, this hits too close to home for me: I won't be watching it.

The optimism with which Zs should be welcoming each of their

---

162 "Stress in America: Generation Z," Stress in America Survey, American Psychological Association, October 2018, https://www.apa.org/news/press/releases/stress/2018/stress-gen-z.pdf.

163 Christina Walker, "10 Years. 180 School Shootings. 356 Victims," CNN, 2019, https://www.cnn.com/interactive/2019/07/us/ten-years-of-school-shootings-trnd/.

school days is under constant erosion from evidence of decline and crisis. In 2020, police killed more than 1,000 people in the streets and police violence has been increasing every year.[164] If we don't reverse our current carbon trajectory, we may reach the ecological point of no return. As of the writing of this book, the global pandemic has killed well over 500,000 Americans and affected 30 million[165]—in a country where 30 million people are without health insurance.[166]

When Zs protest about climate, police violence, school shootings, or universal healthcare, they come away with one question: *Why aren't the older generations doing more?*

MENTAL HEALTH MATTERS

As we've seen, sharing their stories online has given Zs great generational empathy. It has also created shared generational trauma.

Zs are on their devices so much that they can't escape the news cycle. It's messing with their heads. It puts their brains in a constant state of alert, of fight or flight. The human brain has not fundamentally changed for more than 50,000 years. It doesn't know how to process 24/7 danger. It can't separate danger in the real world from perceived danger online. Zs' brains and

164 Tucker Higgins, "These 4 Charts Describe Police Violence in America," CNBC, June 1, 2020, https://www.cnbc.com/2020/06/01/george-floyd-death-police-violence-in-the-us-in-4-charts.html.

165 Lucy Tompkins and Mitch Smith, "COVID-19: US Surpasses 500,000 COVID-19 Deaths, a Monumental Loss," *The New York Times*, April 12, 2021, https://www.nytimes.com/live/2021/02/22/world/COVID-19-coronavirus.

166 Smiljanic Stasha, "Uninsured Americans Stats and Facts 2021: Policy Advice," PolicyAdvice, February 14, 2021, https://policyadvice.net/insurance/insights/how-many-uninsured-americans/.

bodies are in a constant state of fear and uncertainty, and the result is constant stress.

We know that an overly stimulated and constantly stressed brain causes physical changes in the brain and in the body. It's linked to addiction, anxiety, cancer, depression, diabetes, heart disease, and obesity. In our research, well over half of Zs say climate causes them stress or anxiety. The APA has warned that these high levels of eco-anxiety pose a threat to our children and that the failure to take prompt substantive action is an active injustice to them and their mental and physical health.

When Zs were asked about the most common issues they see among their peers, 70 percent said anxiety and depression. Not alcohol or drugs or bullying but mental health.[167] On a positive note, Zs know of their friends' and peers' mental health struggles better than kids in the past because this generation is working to destigmatize mental health: they openly discuss it IRL as well as sharing their individual journeys with anxiety and depression on platforms like TikTok, where the hashtag #MentalHealthMatters has had more than 8 billion views.

There's evidence our wider culture is embracing more open dialogue around mental health, too. Look no further than the 2020 election, when the Trump campaign tried to make Hunter Biden's mental health and drug addiction a character issue. Biden responded, "Mental health is real. Drug addiction is real. I couldn't be more proud of my son. He conquered that;

---

167 Juliana Menasce Horowitz and Nikki Graf, "Most U.S. Teens See
     Anxiety, Depression as Major Problems," Pew Research Center, May
     30, 2020, https://www.pewresearch.org/social-trends/2019/02/20/
     most-u-s-teens-see-anxiety-and-depression-as-a-major-problem-among-their-peers/.

he's a success story"—to the applause of both Democrats and Republicans.

According to a National Institutes of Health (NIH) study, one in three thirteen- to eighteen-year-olds will experience an anxiety disorder. The number of teens who say they have recently experienced depression increased 59 percent in the last decade, and teen suicide rose 66 percent between 2007 and 2017.

The NIH attributes the rise in anxiety, depression, and suicide to three things: the state of the world, social media, and the pressure to succeed. And these findings cut across all gender, racial, and socioeconomic lines. Although certainly some Zs are exposed to more trauma than others, no Z, regardless of race or affluence, is immune. They share the collective trauma of our time, so it affects all of them.

Meanwhile, the pressure to succeed has grown as schools and the job market have both become more competitive. When Zs were asked to identify the main source of pressure, 61 percent of teens pointed to getting good grades, while only 6 percent said pressure to drink alcohol, and only 4 percent said pressure to use drugs.[168] When I was a teen, sure we studied and cared about good grades, but school rankings, test scores, and college admissions were not as competitive as they are now. Our parents and administrators were more focused on helping us combat "peer pressure" to drink and do drugs. We were the DARE (Drug Abuse Resistance Education) generation, which frankly, riled up the adults much more than it did us kids.

COVID has only made things more intense, creating a world in

---

168 Ibid.

which teenagers have even more uncertainty and higher levels of stress and depression. In an APA study that asked people if they felt their mental health had worsened during COVID, 28 percent of boomers said yes, as did 31 percent of millennials. But 46 percent of Gen Z adults—almost half—said their mental health had deteriorated during the pandemic. Zs are also most likely to report symptoms of depression; in the two weeks before the survey, more than seven in ten said they had been so tired that they just sat around and did nothing, that they found it hard to stick properly to tasks or concentrate, or that they felt lonely, miserable, or unhappy.[169]

Not only have Gen Zs suffered the greatest collective mental health decline as a result of COVID, but the number of eighteen-to twenty-nine-year-olds living at home during the pandemic was 52 percent.[170] This is the highest percentage ever recorded (for comparison, it was 48 percent at the height of the Great Depression). This at an age when Zs want to be building their own lives.

The unemployment rate for workers aged sixteen to twenty-four years old is at a high of 24.4 percent, and it was reported that up to one-third of Zs lost their jobs between March and April 2020.[171] Most college graduates during the pandemic had their job offers pulled out from under them. Evidence suggests that

169 "Stress in America," American Psychology Association, March 2021, https://www.apa.org/news/press/releases/stress.

170 Richard Fry, Jeffrey S. Passel, and D'Vera Cohn, "A Majority of Young Adults in the U.S. Live with Their Parents for the First Time since the Great Depression," Pew Research Center, September 9, 2020, https://www.pewresearch.org/fact-tank/2020/09/04/a-majority-of-young-adults-in-the-u-s-live-with-their-parents-for-the-first-time-since-the-great-depression/.

171 Elise Gould and Melat Kassa, "Young Workers Hit Hard by the COVID-19 Economy: Workers Ages 16–24 Face High Unemployment and an Uncertain Future," Economic Policy Institute, October 14, 2020, https://www.epi.org/publication/young-workers-COVID-recession/.

graduating during a recession or not having a job upon graduation translates to a long-term trajectory of lower earnings, lower wealth, and delayed milestones such as homeownership.

Zs don't need a crystal ball to see this puts their potential future in further jeopardy.

On top of that, they are entering a workforce with $1.6 trillion in student debt[172] and 17.8 million Americans unemployed.[173]

The uncertainty is daunting. And it impacts younger Zs as well. More than half of thirteen- to seventeen-year-olds said the pandemic made planning for their future feel impossible.[174] These are middle schoolers and high schoolers who don't feel able to look forward to their adulthood. We have to take notice of this loss of hope; we have to ask ourselves what comes next.

THEY'RE JUST KIDS

We need to see Gen Z as the kids and teenagers they are. We sometimes forget because they have grown up so fast, taking on such responsibility and rightly demanding equal voice and equal respect.

But beneath their tough words and actions, these are kids and teenagers who are still trying to figure out so much in their own lives, let alone taking on this additional burden. As a society, we

172 Abigail J Hess, "How Student Debt Became a $1.6 Trillion Crisis," CNBC, June 12, 2020, https://www.cnbc.com/2020/06/12/how-student-debt-became-a-1point6-trillion-crisis.html.

173 Heather Long, "Nearly 8 Million Americans Have Fallen into Poverty since the Summer," *The Washington Post*, December 16, 2020, https://www.washingtonpost.com/business/2020/12/16/poverty-rising/.

174 "Stress in America 2020: A National Mental Health Crisis," American Psychological Association, 2020, https://www.apa.org/news/press/releases/stress/2020/report-october.

need to do more to support them both in advocating for their causes and in better supporting their mental and physical health.

To me, it seems as if we have failed to protect their future planet. And we have failed to provide a safe, stable society that would have allowed this generation to have the childhood many of us had. Or the systems to help them transition into a viable adult livelihood. This is why I have written this book: so we can all see the world through their eyes. So we can more clearly see our own failings but also the tremendous opportunities this inflection point provides for our shared future: for the future of capitalism, the climate, diversity, education, gender, politics, and work.

Just as Zs have created a digital world of shared empathy that erases barriers, I hope this book serves to create a broader world of shared empathy that transcends generations.

Zs are begging for us to listen to them, to see their vision, and join them in the work.

Conclusion

BEING A GEN Z ALLY

Now that you've reached the end of the book, I hope that you see Zs more clearly: as the regular kids and teenagers that they are but dropped into the most complicated plotline of our lifetimes.

We were all teenagers once and most likely felt misunderstood by older generations. Like we had big ideas and plans for our future that weren't being taken seriously. It's been a complaint of young people forever.

Some of this is just more of the same. But it's also very different because these times are very different.

Coming of age at such a disruptive time has made the divide between Zs and other generations feel exponentially greater. Older generations didn't grow up on an Earth that is burning and where students are being shot in school. We didn't have phones that connected us 24/7 to our peers, creating such a unified generation with its own culture and voice.

Most adults today feel as if the biggest divide in the United States is political: left versus right.

Zs will tell you that the biggest divide in the country is generational.

To Zs, even millennials are old and *different*. They grew up in a bubble that doesn't exist today. Generation We isn't the same. They are not the teenagers of the past but the product of unique factors that have made them protagonists in the most critical movements of our time.

And they feel alone. As if the rest of us are locked in our echo chambers and indoctrinated into systems that are no longer working...but we can't see it. And we can't hear the Zs telling us.

You may have heard of "allyship," a concept that Zs actively embrace which reached the mainstream during the racial justice movement in summer 2020. Allyship calls members of a dominant group to advance the interests of a less dominant group but not by taking over. Instead, by showing up and elevating *their* voices.

Zs are good at this, showing up for each other but handing the microphone to the people most impacted: to their Asian, Black, immigrant, LGBTQ+, or otherwise marginalized peers. Zs know the power of numbers and that when people with privilege, position, or power support a movement, it gains credibility and momentum.

They believe silence is complicity.

Anyone over the age of twenty-four can be an ally to Zs. We just have to really listen to them and their ideas. Seek to understand their unique position at this point in time. Show up and support them.

Most of us have more privilege, position, and power than teenagers. We're valuable allies.

As I said at the beginning of this book, their issues are our issues—they impact *all* of us (though they impact Zs and the generations that will come after them disproportionately). Here's what we can do to be better allies in building our shared future.

WHAT TO DO
1. LISTEN AND LEARN

Zs don't feel they get our respect. That we discount them as being too young to understand how "complicated" climate issues or political or racial dynamics are. After working with Zs, however, I know this to be untrue. In fact, I think they often see our systems more clearly than we do, through a purer lens unadulterated by decades of conditioning. We're the frogs swimming unawares as the pot comes to a boil, and the Zs have just come on the scene yelling for us to jump out.

I was compelled to write this book after working with Zs and being blown away by their savvy understanding, by their ideas, and by their clarity of vision for what's possible. They might not have as much life experience, but their shared digital epicenter gives them a more diverse perspective than many of us have. It's the power of all those shared stories and shared discourse.

Listen to them. You may also be blown away.

And don't be afraid to learn. Don't be afraid to ask questions of them. Don't be afraid to get it wrong. To say the wrong thing, to get canceled, to misappropriate, to use the wrong pronoun. Zs *want* so badly for us to engage with them in meaningful dialogue.

So don't treat them like kids or like teenagers of the past. They're different.

2. GET UNCOMFORTABLE

Redefining gender, remaking capitalism, defunding or reforming the police—Generation We understands that many of their most popular ideas seem entirely radical to older generations and sometimes terrifying. That's why they see the generational divide as larger than any political divide, because Zs are pretty unified in their positions but often feel at odds with their elders.

The idea of allyship, of giving Zs our support, is all about leaning into discomfort. It's about being willing to have uncomfortable conversations that challenge us, that we weren't willing to have before. To talk about how our own social conditioning has shaped us. To look at our personal contributions to our climate crisis, to our political division, to systemic racism.

There is evidence that as we get older, we get more comfortable with the status quo. We must realize that this can make us part of the problem. None of our systems are perfect. We need to be constantly questioning, looking around to see what's working and what we can do better.

As I've said over and over, Zs are not idealists; they are hardened realists who are driven by evidence. Like Zs, we have to be willing to look at things honestly and call BS when something is not working.

Millennial culture gave rise to the idea of "safe spaces," creating bubbles to shut out anything that might upset or "trigger" our young people. Zs have grown up in the real world and favor what they call brave spaces: holding spaces for uncomfortable conversations between diverse people with a broad range of perspectives. This is what they do on TikTok every day. And why they love it.

Zs want to invite older generations into their brave spaces. But they don't feel we're willing to have the same hard conversations. We need to have them. That's where the understanding happens. That's where the change happens.

Getting uncomfortable is the price of being an ally.

3. SEE OUR SHARED HUMANITY

This entire book is about one generation, the Zs. As I said at the beginning, studying a generation is instructive in making us mindful of where we've come from and more intentional about our future. But my real goal is to create shared empathy and understanding across generations.

Our childhoods are different. Our upbringings are different. The world we entered as young adults, very different. But Zs have shown us how difference can be precisely what reminds us of our shared humanity and be used to unite us.

Zs complain that we demean their social media usage. We incorrectly generalize being on their phones as a narcissistic preoccupation that is solely about taking selfies and posting dance videos. As we've seen, much of Zs' social media usage is very purposeful. When it comes to most of the progress I've talked about in this book, social media is the room where it happened.

There is a huge communication divide caused by different social media platforms. Older generations mock Gen Z for getting their news from TikTok, but Zs deliberately choose that platform because it provides a broad range of perspectives and diverse discourse, not an echo chamber. Meanwhile, Zs mock older generations for their use of Facebook and insular social media circles that keep us in our own corners.

Following some of the most divisive years in the political history of our nation, wouldn't we all agree that focusing on what unites rather than divides us would be productive? That it's our diversity of people, experiences, and perspectives that can create an exponentially wiser, stronger, and more empathetic collective?

That our diversity could be our nation's superpower?

4. GIVE THEM REPRESENTATION

Just as we talked about the difference between tokenism and true representation, we need to give Zs true representation and voice, in their educational institutions, in our communities, companies, movements, and our politics.

We tend to hold Zs at arm's length, as what twenty-three-year-old Evan Malbrough calls "a constituency to be managed" rather than a constituency to be truly embraced and integrated. It's because their ideas and tactics challenge us. Frankly, it's easier to discount them. It's easier to stick with the status quo.

The oldest Zs turned twenty-four in 2021. The youngest were only nine or ten. Regardless, they have a unique perspective that deserves a seat at the table. And that means we need to listen to their concerns at the dinner table. Incorporate their ideas into our evolving educational system. Engage with them at both the local and national political level. Invite them into the boardroom to understand their evolving priorities (your business will suffer if you don't).

At ZSpeak, we connect Zs directly with corporate, governmental, and organizational leaders to collaborate on future opportunities and solutions. Other companies are doing the same. Nerf named Sophie Jamison as its Chief TikTok Officer in April 2021. A college junior with 1.8 million followers of her @Nerfers101 TikTok account, she is paid $10,000 a month to help develop, try, and promote Nerf products. Triller is a fast-growing, AI-driven music and video platform, with sights to become the next TikTok. So who did it hire as its Chief Strategy Officer? Eighteen-year-old Josh Richards. As a creator with 25 million TikTok followers, Richards understands what creators want and need and how to build a competitive platform.

That's true representation, and everyone benefits.

5. GET YOUR ACTIVIST ON

Zs are all about bold action. They're pragmatic enough to see that the incrementality of the past is not creating the change we need, so they're not afraid to make big moves.

They're not afraid to speak the truth. They're not afraid to call BS. They're not afraid to call out systems and actors, whoever they may be. But they're also not afraid to be wrong or to learn and adapt as they go. They take bold action because they feel the real enemy is inaction. Don't be put off and scared by their boldness. Be fired up by their boldness. Let it inspire you to have more courage to speak the truth, to put yourself out there, to have a strong voice, to stand up.

Get your activist on.

Generation We know this stuff is easy to say but hard to achieve. They judge their elders harshly for believing that civic responsibility means showing up and voting every couple of years. They see that as passive citizenship. Democracy is a verb and progress requires constant work. Zs' activism is not going away. As we see with Black Lives Matter, activism is an ongoing imperative that spreads over weeks, months, and years.

Generation We wants older generations to join them. To show up at BLM protests. At climate strikes. At marches for gun regulation. They know our privilege and position and power will move us all further faster.

And activism doesn't just mean marching. As eighteen-year-old Megan Chen says, "Every single person has a circle of influence around them, and those people have their circle, and it builds into a whole community." Everyone can listen and engage and act within one's own circle.

THE SEQUEL

Within the arc of history, I reflect on this moment, a moment when it does feel the normal flow of time is catching, hesitating, when it feels we have the potential to shift directions.

The pandemic year, 2020, certainly did feel like an inflection point that exposed our flaws, but it also raised our collective consciousness. When we look back at this juncture in the larger trajectory of our shared humanity, what do we want to see?

Generation We is all about collective action. What would happen if 3 billion Zs were joined by 5 billion Z allies? What could we change in our climate progression? What power could capitalism have to improve our world? How might representation be different in our media, in our organizations, in our politics? How might the next generation grow up differently, in schools safe from violence, streets safe from racial injustice, with the ability to dress and act and love as they wish?

As I've said throughout this book, it's not that Zs were born extraordinary: it's that this time has called on them to be extraordinary. But what if this time has called on ALL of us to be extraordinary? To bring our very best selves and our very best ideas forward?

When someone picks up this book in ten years, what will our world look like? How will we have spent this critical decade?

We all get to start writing the sequel to this book together. Beginning now.

Let's make it a good one.

Acknowledgments

It is not lost on me, the incredible privilege of putting this book out into the world.

What a rich culture we would have if every person could share their story: their message to the world. I know that not everyone can, and that this is a gift.

To that end, this book was really never meant to be about me but to elevate the voices of a generation. It is my hope that you all feel closer to these remarkable young people through their stories and their vision of what's possible. It has been my honor to represent them, and I hope they'll feel I've done them justice.

Being that I am not a Z myself, I am indebted to the thousands of Zs who shared their ideas with me, especially the young people featured in the book who entrusted me with their very real and vulnerable feelings about growing up in today's world. I don't think I had their courage at that age.

Most of all, I'm indebted to my ZSpeak team (who are all Zs), led by the irrepressible twenty-three-year-old Kate Graham, who was my "Z conscience" and BS meter since the conception of this book. Aiden, Emma, Lauren, Mary Grace, Megan: thank you for all of your ideas, your hard work, and for keeping me honest throughout. This book would not have the authenticity, nuance, and truth it does without you. To Chris McGahay, my partner at Global Mosaic, thanks for believing this was possible and graciously giving me the space to make it happen by keeping everything humming.

Huge shout-out to my publishing team, who from our very first meeting shared the urgency of my message and went beyond to bring it into the world—especially to my editorial team led by Tim Cooke for the many months of late-night and weekend calls between London and Chicago.

This book feels like a culmination of the first fifty years of my life, of my work to date and the people who have helped make me who I am. To Mom and Dad, my family, and those fierce Czech immigrant roots: you raised me to believe I could do anything if I worked tirelessly at it, and I couldn't have holed up for the past year without that ethic—thank you. (Incidentally, I hope you feel the encyclopedias you purchased on loan when I was a baby finally provided a decent ROI!)

This book was largely a solitary pursuit. For a year of COVID, I sheltered at home, mostly alone, researching and writing, day after day, night after night. As for most of us, it was an incredibly isolating, lonely, and often tedious period. But in retrospect, it was that stillness and introspection that gave birth to this book and the space to write it. From a pre-COVID life crisscrossing the globe to a year in solitary confinement at home writing: life doesn't let us get too comfortable. Switch it up. Try something new. Be uncomfortable. Thanks for the lesson.

To my chosen "sisters" whom I have collected through each life stage—you are my community, my aspen grove; you keep me watered and nourished and supported and I love that our roots are all tangled up together on this life's journey. You always push me to grow taller than I think is possible. Thank you for helping me see what I'm capable of when I can't.

There are a couple of special people who came into my life in the past year as if on cue, stoking my creative spirit, challenging my thinking, pushing me in all the right ways, and sometimes just making me a much-needed coffee, or cocktail, or body-nourishing meal. You made me and my book better—you know who you are.

Finally, to my two loves, Isabel and Siena, my daughters and two favorite Zs. It was indeed your blindingly bright spirits, tireless curiosity, defiant voices, uncompromising ideas and demand to make change that opened my mind to new ways of thinking. That helped me see my own social conditioning and limitations as a Gen Xer. Your inspiration and energy are infused into every page of this book. As I send you off into the world over the next two years, I know you will continue to do good things.

Let us all continue to do good things.

With gratitude,
AnneMarie

About the Author

As a kid, AnneMarie could be found devouring *National Geographic* and the country profiles in her parents' *Encyclopedia Britannica,* imagining the cultures she would see and study when she was older.

She loves that she got to create her dream job when she grew up, founding and running two companies that specialize in culture:

Global Mosaic (in 2002) and ZSpeak (in 2020). Happily, she now spends her days crisscrossing the country and the globe immersing in new ways of thinking and living, speaking and writing about societal evolution.

AnneMarie is a lifelong student of culture, spending her 20s running global projects for multi-nationals around the world, living on four continents (Asia, Europe, North America and South America) and leading initiatives across more than 50 countries. She served as SVP of Global Strategic Planning at BBDO and VP of Global Strategic Planning at Leo Burnett.

She returned to academia in her early 30s, studying the modern and historical drivers of cultural, economic and political transition, and earning a graduate degree in economics at the University of Chicago with highest honors.

AnneMarie is a sought-after cultural expert and thought-leader, consulting with the world's largest companies, start-up founders, cultural/educational institutions, non-profit organizations, governments and presidential candidates.

Proud to be called a social agitator, AnneMarie believes in continually pushing us forward to do better. She's passionate about the cultural and generational movements shaping our world, and loves to speak and write about what comes next in our evolution.

She lives in Chicago with her two teenage daughters, two dogs and two fish, where she is happiest when writing, reading, making music, crafting great cocktails from her herb garden and eating fresh veggies from the farmer's market.

CPSIA information can be obtained
at www.ICGtesting.com
Printed in the USA
LVHW051748020123
736288LV00002B/182

9 781544 523132